# Teaching Academic Writing in English

## A Practical Approach


Kriti Gulati

*Foreword by*

**Prof. M.P. Sinha**

Former Professor and Head
Department of English
CSJM University, Kanpur (U.P.)



**ATLANTIC**

**PUBLISHERS & DISTRIBUTORS (P) LTD**

Published by

**ATLANTIC**

**PUBLISHERS & DISTRIBUTORS (P) LTD**

7/22, Ansari Road, Darya Ganj, New Delhi-110002
Phones : +91-11-40775252, 40775214, 23273880, 23275880
Fax: +91-11-23285873
Web: www.atlanticbooks.com
E-mail: orders@atlanticbooks.com

**Branch Office: Chennai**
Phones : +91-44-48531784, 28291383
E-mail: chennai@atlanticbooks.com



Printed & bound in India by Atlantic Print Services

# Foreword

It is a great pleasure for me to write a foreword for Kriti's book entitled *Teaching Academic Writing in English: A Practical Approach*. Herself a teacher and educator with a brilliant academic record, she began her career as a teacher trainer at the British Council. As a trainer, she has trained teachers in Kerala, Tamil Nadu, Uttar Pradesh, Maharashtra, Karnataka, Assam, Punjab, and Madhya Pradesh. Besides, she has written teachers' training materials for the British Council, Oxford University Press, and Cambridge University Press. At present she is engaged in teacher training programs with various educational institutions in different parts of the country. I am sure that the book will be of immense help to the entire community of English teachers in India who wish to identify and crystallize the areas to be elaborated, while concentrating on developing academic writing skills in school children. As a reference book it is indeed a panacea for all problems and issues confronted by teachers of English at different levels as well as an unfailing resource text for teachers of English as an Additional Language in schools that have opted for the International Baccalaureate course or the Cambridge International General Certificate of Secondary Education. Teachers preparing their students to pursue studies abroad will also be benefited by the contents of this book which deal exhaustively with all the conceivable aspects of academic writing that a student might wish to refer to or explore with the prime purpose of faring well in school examinations.

With regard to students who have opted for international boards the criteria for assessment are different from those applied to the traditional and regular courses. A thorough comprehension of the ideas and notions offered as well as a statement of the content assimilation is expected of the learners, but often, the inability of students to fruitfully convey their learning becomes an area of concern and it is this issue that has been dealt with here.

The modes of Content and Language Integrated Learning (CLIL) and Language Across the Curriculum (LAC) are generally considered to be potent ways of teaching content-writing as well as of effecting communication of what is imbibed. Teaching through CLIL incorporates content as well as language targets, sometimes with the help of a co-teacher, to concentrate on the language goals. But, there is a perpetual conflict regarding the priority for one of the two prime aspects, namely, language and content. If students are made to focus on language, they may lose their grip on content and if centrality is endowed to content language may not meet the bar.

The areas of learning which need to be accessed by students for the acquisition of expertise in academic language, which is a pre-requisite for admission to a course in Humanities or Science stream, in India and abroad, have been clearly identified and elucidated in this book. The information and knowledge provided in the text will facilitate all aspirants who wish to join colleges and universities primarily in countries like America, Britain, and Australia. The principal thrust in this kind of language teaching is on enabling learners to understand and grasp text-book content written in academic language as well as on affording precise, formal, and coherent texts. So, a command of academic writing would ensure in one the ability to provide a written composition that is at once linguistically correct and socially proper, for context, as Dell Hymes believes, is vital and cannot be ignored or overlooked. Both the situational and the verbal context of statements have a significant role to play in language constructs. "Communicative competence" as Hymes conceives of it is what a language learner endeavours to attain. This book is a discriminating guide to the acquisition of competence in "Academic English", which is precise in expression and grammar, and cohesive in thought. I wish the author academic returns in terms of appreciation and response.

**Prof. (Dr.) M.P. Sinha**
Former Professor and Head
Department of English
CSJM University, Kanpur (U.P.)

# Preface

When I started teaching English as an Additional Language teacher in an international school four years back, I realized that though the students were required to know and understand Academic Language and use it in their study related to oral and written endeavours, they possessed no real clarity as to what Academic Language was or how it was different from the commonly used social language that is heard and used all around. The common question asked was, "How is it that a child who speaks so fluently in English is unable to present his thoughts, opinions, and reasoning using appropriate language in the assessments, primarily in writing?"

The most amusing discovery was that though teachers expect students to use Academic Language in the work they produce, they themselves are not sure what Academic Language entails and how students are to be taught the language and exposed to it. On observing some subject teaching classes in the course of my work, I learned that teachers do not really use much Academic Language while teaching except when using the terms specific to their subjects. Barring some teachers, as is always the case, most academicians are neither explicitly teaching nor exposing the students to the kind of language they need to reproduce in their output texts. In my endeavour to address the need for teaching Academic Language, I evaluated several books that were available for the study. I read Stephen Bailey's *Academic Writing: A Practical Guide for Students* as well as *Academic Writing: A Handbook for International Students.* I also looked at Derek Soles' *The Essentials of Academic Writing.* These books are incontestably great resources, yet, they did not give me answers to my questions. What are the different types of essays that need to be written in school? What are the elements that children need to be aware of and know the application of? How can teachers develop the language students are expected to use in their essays? What is the effective method of teaching 'writing academic essays' in schools? Hence, the need for a book which focuses on apprising students of Academic Language, the various essay formats to be used and other important elements required to be known was felt. The need for a book that guides teachers on what they must teach and how they can teach it to receive desired results was also perceived.

Having assessed the requirement for a book with a lucid, precise and simple explanation of Academic Language, particularly Academic Writing, since most educational input as well as output is in the written form, I started searching for books by some well-known authors. I read quite a few books which enlightened me on major theories in the field and made me aware of the elaborate discussions on concerned topics and issues. However, I found none that approached Academic Writing directly. It was then that I decided to write a book that would address the understanding and teaching of Academic Writing upfront.

In this venture, I have elaborated only on Academic Writing in a detailed and focused manner. I have dealt with all aspects of Academic Writing in a bid to make it an unprecedented and useful resource for all teachers as well as students who might want to improve their Educational Writing skills through self-study. It guides both students and teachers on areas of high importance and seeks to build an understanding of the varied kinds of writing that they are required to churn out for a deeper connection with the expectations. However, there are areas which have been dealt with at a cursory level. This is because these areas have complete books dealing with the concerned topics explicitly and I believe repeating the same information would be a waste of space.

In this book I have drawn upon all my research on what students and teachers need to know. In addition to interviewing teachers and students personally to understand their current levels in terms of Academic Language, I have analysed their responses and work produced for inputs. Through this book, I have tried to address the queries that have been raised in this regard over the years by students in schools.

I hope this book will provide the much-needed support to all subject teachers as well. I have discussed the approaches to teaching-writing in detail for their benefit and also mentioned some ways in which the different elements of Academic Writing can be taught.

Happy learning and teaching!

**Kriti Gulati**

# Acknowledgements

This book is a result of long hours of toil, research, and study. Being able to put all of your learning, experience, and understanding in one place to be shared with a larger audience is an exhilarating and highly satisfying achievement. In this journey of learning and sharing, I could not have succeeded without the unstinted support of my parents, particularly my mother, Dr. Reena Mitra, who is an academician of high repute herself, my husband, Sumit Gulati and my children, Kashvi and Milo who lost time with me but never complained. In fact, it was their constant encouragement and understanding that led me to complete this book in good time. I would like to extend a special thank you to my mother who despite her busy and demanding schedule took time out to read my work and give me a feedback on it. I would never have been able to accomplish this piece had it not been for her pushing and guiding me the way she did.

Apart from my immediate family, I would also like to thank my former workplace, Pathways School, Noida, for being my laboratory. I learnt and applied my learning to issues of interest, identified areas of further work, and turned again to application of academic attainment, all in Pathways and with my students. It is this circular course of pursuits that has yielded the fulfilment of my intellectual aspirations. I would like to express my gratitude to Dr. Shalini Advani, the Director at Pathways School, Noida, for having enabled my access to invaluable research material in the form of books available in the school library.

I express my heartfelt gratitude to each individual who walked the path with me and helped me to reach my destination.

# Contents

# 1
# An Introduction to Academic Writing

## The Purpose of this Book

I have been teaching English to adults and children in schools for the past 13 years in different capacities. This book is proposed as an effective solution to the problems of all English teachers in India who struggle to identify the areas to be addressed while trying to develop the Academic writing competence of school children. It is intended to be a reference book and in many ways a resource book for teachers of English as an Additional Language (henceforth EAL) in schools with international boards as well as for teachers who are working to prepare their students to study abroad.

My purpose in writing this book is to provide information on all aspects of Academic Writing that a student needs to know, and a teacher needs to teach so that academic endeavours in school examinations can be more rewarding. Students who study in international boards are academically judged based on different criterion. Knowledge and understanding of conceptual content and communication of the same are assessed severally. It has been commonly noticed in the Indian conditions that though the tutees might be well versed with the content they are unable to amply convey their learning. The reasons for this are many.

The field of education has seen an upheaval of the formal education system. In today's evolved academic order, textbooks have become a little more than reference books. Each topic of study is supplemented with videos made by academicians or scholars which may or may not use 'Academic language'.

Since in India, teachers teaching subjects other than English Literature or Language are not expected or required to have a level of competence in English at which the use of 'Academic Language' becomes a natural language trait, an Indian student's exposure to the stated form of language is limited. Given the circumstances, it becomes imperative that dedicated attention be paid to the teaching of 'Academic Language', either as interwoven with subject teaching as purported through the concepts of Content and Language Integrated Learning (CLIL) or through Language Across the Curriculum (LAC) which are widely understood as effective ways of teaching content along with focus on the language needed to communicate the same, or through remedial courses being offered parallelly to the ongoing education system. While quite a few schools and academic institutions have successfully implemented the content with the language teaching approach effectively, there are many that have not.

To achieve a better understanding and to allow for a higher level of engagement with the current as well as with the upcoming content, I would like to explain the mentioned terms of CLIL and LAC briefly.

The European Commission's (1995) White Paper, "Teaching and Learning: Towards the Learning Society" set the stage for the blooming of the CLIL approach. CLIL replaced existing approaches like, Content Based Instruction (CBI) and Immersion and was launched by UNICOM in 1996. Defining CLIL, Marsh and Langé in Anna Czura's article say,

> CLIL is a generic term and refers to any educational situation in which an additional language, and therefore not the most widely used language of the environment, is used for the teaching and learning of subjects other than the language itself. (Marsh and Langé 2000)

Teaching through CLIL demands that a subject matter teacher has language goals for her/his students just like s/he has content learning goals. Achievement of both goals must be targeted. Several teaching models have been proposed for CLIL. Some require that the same teacher plans and works to achieve both, language as well as content, goals, while others call for co-teaching whereby there is a co-teacher to focus on the language goals. Some schools have an approach whereby they have an EAL teacher attached with every grade. In such a set-up, while the subject matter teacher concentrates on imparting subject knowledge, the EAL teacher co-teaches to focus on teaching, developing and giving practice in the formal language required to communicate the concepts learnt, the evaluation arrived at and the analysis concluded by critically approaching the content exposed to. However, whether this arrangement has borne desired results is debatable.

Christiane Dalton-Puffer in her book, *Discourse in Content and Language Integrated Learning* (2007) beautifully sums up the problems involved in the successful implementation of CLIL. She says,

> A major concern and one of the 'main ongoing challenges' (Snow, 1998, 258) in most forms of CLIL is the relationship between language and content. This relationship, despite the presence of the word 'integrated' in CLIL is characterized by a good deal of tension and sometimes conflict between the two areas... the conflict is about the primacy of one aspect over the other. Interestingly, the more frequently articulated voice is that of the content teacher concerned about the consequences of foreign language use on the students' eventual knowledge of the subject.... (p. 5)

The problems in implementing CLIL are manifold. One, the content teacher may not be comfortable leaving the floor for the language teacher. There is a conflict of domain that ensues. This can present an unpleasant work situation and affect the learning and teaching environment adversely. Another aspect is the implication on the students' dilemma. If the students focus on the language, they may lose out on mastery over the content taught and vice versa. This threat always looms large on the horizon for the students and more often than not, they decide in favour of content. Their choice is often determined by the system of examinations that we have, which gives primacy to knowledge over language.

Coming to LAC or Language Across Content, which for all practical purposes, is the precursor to CLIL which emerged in Britain in the 1970s as "a whole-school approach to address the language and literacy needs of students studying in different subject area" (Angel M.Y. Lin, p. 6).

Having been a part of the schooling order in India for a long time, I have come to the conclusion that for CLIL or LAC to become truly effective, it is important that teachers of all subjects be equally proficient in the use of English language which is the language of instruction in most schools in the country. Since this prerequisite demands time and money of massive proportions, it becomes an almost impossible goal. The alternative to this proposition is the English as an Additional Language program which schools offer to help and support students who do not have the level of English language proficiency called for by the higher education organizations abroad. This book offers a streamlined and practical approach to teaching Academic Language in such EAL programs. A knowledge of the topics and areas, which, must be necessarily disseminated among the students so as to adequately equip them with a command over academic language needed for the purpose of seeking admission into a humanities or scientific stream abroad has been elaborately covered in this book.

## Emergence of Academic Writing

Colonization is recognized as one of the most important reasons for the spread of English Language. The members of colonized nations wanted to learn the language of the colonizer so that they could gain a position of favour in the system. English found root in India during the British Rule. The British went back but left behind a rich legacy of language and culture. The same can be said of all the nations and areas that the English ruled over in the past. Gradually, as many English-speaking nations, mainly America, gained prominence as prosperous states, more people in India wanted to learn English for the sake of travel, emigration and in some cases even study. With the opening up of the economic system in 1991, English spread its reach further into the society and established itself as the language of business. Many English-speaking nations began to outsource work to India and a need for an English-speaking workforce was created. Companies began to set up shops in India and the demand for speakers of the English language went up even higher. More and more schools with English as their medium of educational instruction came up. For adults, to give them a chance to 'move up' in life despite their schooling in the local language, English language schools mushroomed in every nook and corner of the country. In fact, the British Council, which is an academic governing body in Great Britain, set up shop as an English language school in India. The market for English language learning has only grown over the decades.

The recent years have seen English transform its image from being the language of business to that of the language of Higher Education. As a result of the major English-speaking countries of the world, primarily America, Britain and Australia, promoting their universities and educational courses with much vigour and promises, students from all over the world started aspiring to join the ever-growing brigade of scholars in the aforementioned countries. Getting admission and then studying in these educational organizations requires a certain level of English language as well as the knowledge of the language used in education, commonly known as 'Academic Language'. It is interesting to note that the desire to join a college in the countries mentioned above and more, has opened the doors of school education to international school boards like the International Baccalaureate (IB) and the Cambridge International General Certificate of Secondary Education (Cambridge IGCSE). These school boards offer themselves as the perfect springboards to advanced education abroad. With the coming in of these organizations into schools of countries whose first language is not English, appeared the demand for learning English as an Additional Language (EAL) alongside the subject curriculum in schools. The primary objective of this genre of language teaching is to equip school students to read and comprehend textbook content which is written using Academic Language as well as to produce texts which have the precision, formality, coherence and cohesion of the same.

As Ian Bruce in his book, *Academic Writing and Genre: A Systematic Analysis* says,

> Central to the mastery of Academic writing is the novice writers' development of discourse competence, particularly in relation to academic prose. This involves writers developing the ability to integrate a wide range of different types of knowledge in order to create extended written discourse that is both linguistically accurate and socially appropriate. (Bruce, p. 1)

Bruce has drawn his theory on Academic writing from his understanding of the term 'communicative competence' coined by Dell Hymes (1972). Hymes introduced this term in response to Chomsky's use of the term 'linguistic competence'. In fact, Chomsky (1965) introduced two related expressions, 'linguistic competence' (the grammar knowledge of a speaker-listener) and 'linguistic performance' (the speaker-listener's actual use of language). Chomsky in his book, *Aspects of the Theory of Syntax*, stated,

> Linguistic theory is concerned primarily with an ideal speaker-listener, in a completely homogeneous speech community, who knows its language perfectly and is unaffected by such grammatically irrelevant conditions as memory limitations, distractions, shifts of attention and interest, and errors (random or characteristic) in applying his knowledge of the language in actual performance. (Chomsky, 3)

While defining his coined phrase above, Chomsky assumes that the sociolinguistic environment of a speaker-listener does not impact his language competence. 'Communicative Competence' was a term which Dell Hymes came up with in 1972 in response to Chomsky's narrow vision of Linguistics. Speaking about Hymes's response, Marianne Celce-Murcia, in her article, "Rethinking the Role of Communicative Competence in Language Teaching" says that while Chomsky believed that language could be learned free of a context, Hymes believed that context was of prime importance. Not only must a learner understand the structure of language constructs but also how the same are used effectively. The latter was possible only in the presence of a context. Though rules of language use can be learnt in isolation, yet to understand the impact of such use and to be able to discern which rule to apply where for maximum effectiveness, one needs a context. The basic thought was that given that English, or for that matter any language, is a mode of communication between people who deal with a variety of situations, it cannot be context free.

Corroborating Hymes' claim that context of language use is important are Campbell and Wales (1970) who offer a new definition of linguistic 'competence' and state,

> .....the ability to produce or understand utterances which are not so much grammatical but, more important, appropriate to the context in which they are made (on this point, the crux of this chapter, see also Schlesinger, 1969). By 'context' we mean both the situational and the verbal context of utterances...an adequate psychology of language must take account not only of the creative aspects of language use but also of the important role played by contextual factors. (pg. 4. Chap. 13. *New Horizons in Linguistics*, Penguin Books, 1970)

In 1983, Canale added another component to the definition of 'Communicative competence', that of discourse competence.

Canale (1983, 1984) described discourse competence as mastery of rules that determine ways in which forms and meanings are combined to achieve a meaningful unity of spoken or written texts. The unity of a text is enabled by cohesion in form and coherence in meaning. Cohesion is achieved by the use of cohesion devices (e.g. pronouns, conjunctions, synonyms, parallel structures etc.) which help to link individual sentences and utterances to a structural whole. The means for achieving coherence, for instance repetition, progression, consistency, relevance of ideas etc., enable the organisation of meaning, i.e. establish a logical relationship between groups of utterances. (p. 97. *Defining Communicative Competence*, Metodika Vol. 8, br. 1, 2007.)

The concept of Academic writing is essentially derived from the concept of 'Communicative Competence'. Communicative competence comprises the following four elements as identified by Michael Canale and Merrill Swain (1980) and Canale (1983);

1. **Grammatical competence** which includes the knowledge of phonology (the study of pronunciation), orthography (the practice of correct spellings), vocabulary (knowledge of words and expressions to communicate appropriately and meaningfully), word formation (morphology) and sentence formation (syntax).
2. **Sociolinguistic competence** refers to the ability of a speaker-listener to be aware of the sociocultural use of language and use the same appropriately for effective communication. The language user should know which grammatical form to use for which communicative function in which sociolinguistic situation.
3. **Discourse competence** refers to a user's ability to use language to produce cohesive and coherent texts to communicate meaningfully.
4. **Strategic competence** refers to the user's ability to use compensatory strategies in case of grammatical or sociolinguistic or discourse failure. It calls for the use of devices such as reference sources, grammatical and lexical paraphrase, requests for repetition, clarification, slower speech, or problems.

However, the study of Academic writing, mainly involves discourse competence. It also involves grammatical competence since accuracy is important for academic communication. The other two competencies, namely, sociolinguistic, and strategic are concerned with the production skill of language, speaking.

## An Overview of the Book

This book has been carefully planned to cover the important aspects required to be known for a practical teaching and learning of Academic writing. I have focused on 'Academic Writing' in view of the fact that this is the more important productive skill since admissions to colleges and universities as well as examination grades are primarily based on what is written in response to questions posed. I have deliberately kept the historical and origin theories of concepts discussed at minimalistic levels except where elaboration was absolutely necessary for a complete understanding of the notion being taught to maintain the practicality and comprehensibility of the book to the students and teachers of Indian origin and others whose first language is not English.

Having provided some information on the content, usage and distinctive aspects of 'Academic Language' which might help an academician identify its presence or absence in a scholarly text in chapter 2, there is an elaborate discussion on the features of 'Academic Language' in chapter 3. When reading to understand this genre of language, it is imperative that readers are made aware of what constitutes 'Academic Language' in considerable detail. Keeping in mind the fact that this book could be used by students for self-study, I have used multiple examples and contrastive analysis to bring home the features that make an instance of language academic. For teachers too it is important to know what aspects of language to consider while teaching to develop 'Academic Language' among a set of students, as such thought lends clarity and flow to the process of teaching and learning. The mentioned knowledge also allows for an improved comprehension of heard and read academic texts to which exposure is provided. Chapter 4 discusses the organization of content in a written academic text which is determined by the subject it is associated with. Scientific subjects follow a different format from the subjects related to the humanities. Even in humanities, the purpose for writing the essay affects the organization of the information being presented. Each format has a well-defined structure and use of language. These aforementioned aspects are discussed in depth and with relevant and relatable examples for the Indian audience. Chapter 5 talks about the different genres of Academic writing and explains the characteristics, structure and use of language in each. If one is aware of what a category of text entails, it is relatively easy for him or her to identify the purpose of a text and engage with it appropriately at an expected level.

After a discussion of the basic elements of 'Academic Writing', this book delves deeper into the topic in the following chapters. Since the concepts of cohesion and coherence along with the use of language are important notions required to know in order to understand and practice Academic writing with expertise, chapter 6, provides detailed information on them. The two aspects have been defined in the respective chapter and the devices that allow for bringing them into motion in a text are well elaborated upon with the help of contrastive analysis and adequate examples. Teaching 'Academic Writing' has always been a challenge for EAL teachers. It could be as a result of the jagged language proficiency profile of the students or the vast number of elements to be covered. To place some part of the connected anxiety at ease, this book in chapter 7, discusses how the process approach can be fruitfully used to develop 'Academic Writing' skills in students. The chapter also talks about the product approach to teaching writing. Referencing is one of the most important components of academic pieces. It is important to give credit to authors and writers who have informed another piece of writing. Chapter 8 gives an overarching account of the referencing formats that are commonly used by schools and can be chosen from. In keeping with the perennial adage, "Honesty is the best policy", which now has become an important academic practice, the book concludes by talking about plagiarism. I believe it is important for teachers and students to understand what plagiarism is and what it involves. Clarity on this front will go a long way in avoiding the practice in academic circuits.

## Going all the Way and Back

For many years after Independence, the erstwhile colonial nations along with some European countries were swept over by the omnipresent existence of British English. There was stress on the learning and teaching of the Queen's English and accuracy was of prime importance. Anything not in keeping with the 'Standard English' (British or American) was regarded as an error (Selinker 1972; 1992). Gradually the changes in the approaches to English language learning started becoming apparent. Stress on pronunciation receded and the concept of

"World Englishes" (Kachru 1985; 1991) came into existence. The meaning of an 'error' in English language changed as there was no 'standard English' anymore. While diffusing the concept of standard English, Kachru (1985, p. 30) said,

> ...the global diffusion of English has taken an interesting turn: the native speakers of this language seem to have lost the exclusive prerogative to control its standardization; in fact, if current statistics are any indication, they have become a minority. This sociolinguistic fact must be accepted and its implication recognized. What we need now are new paradigms and perspectives for linguistics and pedagogical research and for understanding the linguistic creativity in multilingual situations across cultures.

Supporting Kachru on his concept of World English and his claim that the native speakers can no longer claim ownership of the language, Widdowson (1994, p. 384) said,

> 'How English develops in the world is no business whatsoever of native speakers in England, the United States, or anywhere else. They have no say in the matter, no right to intervene or pass judgment. They are irrelevant. The very fact that English is an international language means that no nation can have custody over it. To grant such custody of the language is necessarily to arrest its development and so undermine its international status. It is a matter of considerable pride and satisfaction for native speakers of English that their language is an international means of communication. But the point is that it is only international to the extent that it is not their language. It is not a possession which they lease out to others, while retaining the freehold. Other people actually own it.'

The impact of this change was worldwide. Accuracy, which was a concept associated with the theory of standard English, took a back seat. Structures spoken and written to communicate were acceptable so long as they communicated meaning with little impediment. Teaching of grammar was no longer impressed upon. It was replaced with the theory of language skills. Students were exposed to written and listening texts to develop language proficiency. An example is that international boards do not call for a structured and explicit teaching of grammar. They impress more on the development of critical thinking and life skills.

Like in the case of every development, this development too had positive and negative implications. A positive implication was mainly felt in what Kachru (1971) calls the 'outer circle and 'expanding circle' countries. More and more people could take to English as a language of communication without the stress of being 'accurate'. The culture of accuracy had been replaced with that of communicability. English language expanded its reach to more and more people and gradually became the lingua franca of the world. On the other side, as accuracy and stress on structure, morphology as well as phonology took a hit, the gap between the erstwhile 'standard English' and 'commonly spoken and written English' widened.

Today when we talk about 'Academic English', we are talking about the precision of expression and grammar, coherence of content and the cohesion of thoughts and ideas. We are referring to register, style and mood of expression. We are alluding to accuracy in diction, structure and morphology. In a way we are attempting to restore the lost order.

## Works Cited

Bruce, Ian. "The Teaching of Academic Writing." *Academic Writing and Genre: A Systematic Analysis*, Continuum, 2008, p. 1.

Campbell, Robin N. and Roger J. Wales. "The Study of Language Acquisition." *New Horizons in Linguistics*, edited by J. Lyons, Penguin Books, 1970, pp. 242-60.

Canale, M. and M. Swain. "Theoretical Bases of Communicative Approaches to Second Language Teaching and Testing." *Applied Linguistics*, I, no. 1, 1 Jan. 1980, pp. 1-47.

Celce-Murcia, M. "Rethinking the Role of Communicative Competence in Language Teaching." *Intercultural Language Use and Language Learning*, edited by Soler Eva Alcón and Jordà Pilar Safont, Springer, 2008, pp. 41-57.

Chomsky, Noam. "Generative Grammars as Theories of Linguistic Competence." *Aspects of the Theory of Syntax*, by MIT P., 1965, p. 3.

Coyle, Do, et al. *CLIL: Content and Language Integrated Learning.* Cambridge University Press, 2013.

Czura, Anna. "CLIL—the European and the Polish Perspective." *Researchgate*, Jan. 2009, www.researchgate.net/publication/303315771_CLIL_-_the_European_and_the_Polish_ perspective.

Dalton-Puffer, Christiane. *Discourse in Content and Language Integrated Learning (CLIL) Classrooms.* John Benjamins, 2007.

Grenfell, Michael. *Modern Languages Across the Curriculum.* RoutledgeFalmer, 2002.

Haase, Christoph, et al. *ELT: New Horizons in Theory and Application.* Cambridge Scholars Publishing, 2015.

Kilickaya, Ferit. "World Englishes, English as an International Language and Applied Linguistics." *English Language Teaching*, Vol. 2, No. 3, 2009.

Lin, Angel M.Y. *Language Across the Curriculum & CLIL in English as an Additional Language (EAL) Contexts 2016: Theory and Practice.* Springer Verlag, Singapore, 2016.

Pride, J.B., et al. "On Communicative Competence." *Sociolinguistics: Selected Readings*, Penguin, 1972, pp. 269-93.

Zarobe, Yolanda Ruiz de, and Jiménez Catalán Rosa María. *Content and Language Integrated Learning Evidence from Research in Europe.* Multilingual Matters Ltd., 2009.

# 2

# The Contours of Academic Language

To understand Academic Writing, it is important to know what Academic language is and how it is different from colloquial or social language. In this regard, an engagement with Jim Cummins' concept of BICS and CALP is imperative. In the same context we will also have a look at Ahmar Mahboob's three-dimensional framework of language variation and get acquainted with the pillars of Academic language, genre and register. These aspects of Academic language are equally relevant. Though there are great debates on genre-analysis by many theorists and academicians, an understanding of what 'Genres' are and how their study impacts development of Academic writing skills is of seminal importance. Apart from this, a deliberation on how the knowledge of genre can be imparted to the students is significant. Additionally, a knowledge of register and its importance in Academic language is indispensable.

In the Indian context, the study of English in most examination boards like CBSE, ICSE and state boards essentially entails an in-depth study of grammar in primary and middle school followed by comprehension exercises and to some extent engagement based on critical thinking with literary texts or extracts thereof. In international boards, which like most Indian boards use English as the medium of instruction, students visit English grammar superficially and are expected to acquire proficiency in spoken and oral English language through immersion in the language. This immersion is expected to happen through the school environment and classroom language use. The irony is that though the interaction in class, academic as well as casual, is mostly in English, the same kind of correspondence outside the class is transacted in the local language. I believe this is because the communication in the local language allows for greater freedom of expression as well as for a better person to person connection. However, this mitigates the impact of English language immersion on the students. Though the intention is to provide a 'full immersion' programme, it ends up being a 'partial' one. So, children do develop proficiency in English, yet not up to the level required for international education. It must be noted here that the kind of English they develop proficiency in is social and not academic. Academic English is almost a different 'genre' of language which has a different style, vocabulary and expression and even a dedicated use.

While we try to understand the difference between social and Academic language, it becomes imperative to talk about Jim Cummins's (1979) BICS (Basic Interpersonal Communication Skills) and CALP (Cognitive Academic Language Proficiency). These concepts were introduced by Cummins to explain the challenges that learners face while studying in a second language. An example could be the learners in India who largely receive academic instruction in English which is their second language.

## BICS and CALP

BICS refers to language which people require for social interaction. This language, students develop through the exposure they receive in their natural environment. If children do not have much exposure to the 'target language' which we identify in this context to be Academic language, they do not develop proficiency in the language at the desired rate and to the required proficiency level. Though movies, blogs, chats, songs, etc. offer exposure to English, it takes a student approximately 2-3 years to develop reasonable fluency in BICS if the language is not available in the regular social surroundings. For example, a lot of children who study in schools with English as the medium of instruction are first generation English learners. They have minimal exposure to English at home and in their daily social relationships. As a result, they do not develop the level of comfort required to choose English as their medium of communication. This leads to a situation where the children talk amongst themselves in the local language and the status quo with target language proficiency remains. Breaking this status quo takes quite some time but it happens. It must be noted that BICS is context embedded and is not very cognitively demanding. It is simple language and the sole purpose is communicating in a social set up.

For example,

Amita: Hi, how was your day at school today?

Nehra: Ok. Not too great.

Amita: What happened? You had a fight with your friends?

Nehra: errrrrrr. Huh.... It's just that we were all talking but Ma'am, identified only me for scolding. She called out my name, asked me to stand up, scolded me and then let me sit with a warning. This even when all've us were talking. After I sat down, there was noise again and Ma'am looked first in my direction. She doesn't even trust me.

Amita: Actually, I think she trusts you the most and does not expect irresponsible behaviour from you. That's why she couldn't believe that you were involved in the 'talking while class' activity. Go talk to your Ma'am tomorrow and explain your point of view.

Nehra: I never thought like that. Thank you big sister! I will definitely go and talk to Ma'am tomorrow.

In the above example we notice that the language used is casual, and highly contextual. It is a conversation, a social interaction and requires the participants to simply respond to each other, share thoughts and opinions or even description of events or situations as required in the course of the conversation.

CALP refers to the language required to engage with academic information that students get exposed to. CALP is required for students to draw conclusions, analyze, evaluate, compare, classify, and synthesize what they read or hear and to communicate their learning and understanding to others through oral or written presentations. This makes the process of studying cognitively very demanding. Hence students need time and focus to develop Academic language. Cummins states that development in CALP to acceptable and effective levels takes five to seven years. In contrast to BICS, CALP is context reduced and mentally more demanding. There are minimal clues to the meaning being conveyed except the words themselves and the language is abstract. For example,

> *Price Elasticity of Supply* is calculated the same way as *Price Elasticity of Demand*. This time, however, it is the percentage change in supply which has to be calculated. Again, it is found by dividing the *change in supply* by the *original supply* and multiplying by 100. Similarly, the percentage change in price is calculated by dividing the *change in price* by the *original price* and multiplying by 100. (Cambridge IGCSE Economics, p. 78)

> The molecules in the gas state above a liquid exert a *vapour pressure. Molecules* will continue to evaporate from the liquid until the pressure reaches a maximum value for the temperature, called the *saturated vapour pressure.* (MYP by Concept 4&5 Chemistry, p. 127)

In both the extracts above, there is no context as such. It is just technical language used to impart subject related knowledge. The expression is precise and style formal.

It has been widely acknowledged that "in today's educational arena, Academic language is central to schooling and is one of the most important factors influencing academic success" (Francis, Rivera, Lesaux, Kieffer, and Rivera, 2006). It is important to mention here that the difference between everyday English and Academic English is quite blurred to the students. Movies, TV shows, social media, etc. being a major source of English language learning, most students are fluent in everyday English but not Academic English. Their exposure to Academic English is limited in every sense. Few of their teachers speak Academic English while teaching. At this juncture, I must mention that apart from the English teachers, few other teachers are expected to have more than a workable knowledge of English in India. Though schools offering International Curriculums are particular in this regard and ensure that most of their teachers are proficient in the concerned language, yet this does not guarantee an inflow of Academic language into the school environment.

Academic language needs to be consciously taught. Before we discuss what could be done to develop Academic language skills, getting clarity on what Academic language denotes and connotes is crucial.

## What is Academic Language?

As distinguished from social language, Academic language is the language of study. It is the language students receive educational information in through textbooks and classroom discussions. It is the language students are expected to use when they write assignments, make oral presentations, write reports or essays. It is essentially the language of academics. Social language on the other hand is the language of social interaction. Academic language is a variety of language which is used for a specific purpose for a specific audience in a context. In the words of Bailey and Heritage (2008; Gottlieb, Katz and Ernst-Slavit, 2009; Schlepperell, 2004),

> Broadly speaking, Academic Language refers to the language used in schools to acquire a new or deeper understanding of the content and to communicate that understanding to others.

Academic language is concise and specific in its expression and uses subject specific jargon. For example, Look at the language for a task from "Cambridge Checkpoint English Coursebook" by Marian Cox on p. 11.

> Look again at the autobiographical texts 1B, 1C and 1D. Work in pairs to collect a list of the things mentioned

in them such as nature, which create the setting for the memory that features in the texts. Think about the setting you will use in your own piece of writing.

To understand this task, the students will have to know the meaning of words like—'autobiographical' and 'setting'. This is an instance of Academic language. What we conclude here is that students need to be able to read, listen, speak, and write in Academic language. This book discusses the sub-skills related to the writing skill only.

An interesting feature of Academic language is that it is developmental in nature. This means that the level of complexity grows with every grade. This also means that the teaching and learning of Academic language works in a layered manner, that is, skills that are taught and developed in one grade build on what has been taught and learned in the previous grade. The development in Academic language in a grade depends on the exposure students receive during the term, in their immediate pedagogical environment, in oral or written form. As children advance in their educational journey, the information they receive through their textbooks and otherwise becomes more and more abstract and dense. The higher classes offer specialized knowledge and to understand and engage with that knowledge students must be equipped adequately and appropriately. Students can receive exposure to Academic language through their textbooks, subject related journals, research papers, academic conferences, symposiums, expert podcasts and live chats and even in class discussions with peers and the teacher on matters of importance related to a discipline. A classroom is the best place to arrange for such meaningful exposure for the students in context.

Academic language can be studied at three levels, discourse, sentence, and word/phrase. The following table has been adapted from Margo Gottlieb and Gisela Ernst-Slavit's table "Dimensions of Academic Language" gives a fair idea on what topics can be covered in the teaching-learning process at each level.

| Levels of Academic Language | Areas of Teaching/Learning |
|---|---|
| Discourse | Text Types<br>Genres<br>Register<br>Voice<br>Organization and Layout<br>Coherence and Cohesion |
| Sentence | Types of sentences—simple, compound, complex, compound-complex<br>Clauses—relative, conditional, etc.<br>Phrases—noun, prepositional, adverbial, adjectival<br>Syntax<br>Nominalization |
| Word/Phrase | Transition words and expressions<br>Idiomatic expressions<br>Connotative meaning Vs. Denotative meaning<br>Synonyms<br>Contextual meaning |

In most cases, the teaching-learning in the smaller classes starts at the word/phrase level and then knowledge is built upon as the children move up the grades.

As we consider the levels of Academic language, let us take a look at the 'Brick and Mortar' approach to teaching vocabulary in Academic language briefly. Susana Durto and Carroll Moran, two academicians studying English language development, introduced the terms "brick" and "mortar" to describe the types of academic vocabulary words. They said 'brick' words are 'subject specific words' meaning those words that we call key terms. Comprehension of these words is important to understand an academic topic. For instance, in Literature words like setting, plot, literary device, etc; In Science, respiration, expiration, inhalation, etc; In History, revolution, overthrow, rebellion, etc. These words are generally taught through various techniques before the topic content is laid out for easier understanding and making connections with the topic. 'Mortar' are words which are common across disciplines. These are words which allow the 'brick' words to be presented meaningfully, words that hold the 'bricks' together. For example, expressions like—although, however, to sum up, implies, contains, supports, etc. It is important for students being trained in Academic language to know 'mortar' vocabulary as well as the 'brick' vocabulary for an effective academic output—oral or written. A good strategy for teaching 'mortar' words is to first identify them in a context and then use them in the discussions conducted for the content in the context. The teacher must use the terms in context as often as possible providing model usage. The teacher must insist on the use of the same in oral or written responses to the questions and tasks set on the topic.

Learning Academic language is not just about knowing and understanding its components. As stated by Margo Gott Lieb and Gisela Ernst-Slavit "It encompasses knowledge about ways of being in the world, ways of acting, thinking, interacting, valuing, believing, speaking and sometimes reading and writing connected to particular identities and social roles" (Gee 1992, p. 73). Continuing in the same strain, lets briefly discuss the roles of Academic language that Zwiers (2008) describes in his book *Building Academic Language: Essential Practices for Content Classrooms, Grades 5-12.* He states that Academic language has 3 roles—to describe complexity, higher order thinking, and abstraction. Zwiers mentions that these three functions overlap and take different forms in each content area and at each grade level. In its role to describe complexity, Academic language is required to explain every complex concept present on a topic as clearly as possible. Every concept has complex concepts and ideas. Academic language uses precise diction and appropriate expression to make them comprehensible. This complexity increases with the grades and is reflected in the Academic language used therein. The next function of Academic language is to describe the 'Higher order thinking skills' like analyzing, synthesizing and evaluating in that order as per Bloom's taxonomy. The final function of Academic language is to describe an abstract concept which is "an idea or relationship that we cannot easily act out, point to or illustrate with images as can often be done in home and social settings" (*Building Academic Language: Essential Practices for Content Classrooms*, p. 25). This primarily involves the concept of words changing meaning with different contexts. For instance, look at the two sentences—'A room with *a view*' and 'He has *a view*'. The meaning of the word 'view' is abstract in the second sentence.

To sum up, to understand Academic language one needs to know the relationship of the speakers or writers involved, the purpose of the communication, the audience and the context in which the conversation is taking place. These concepts can be studied under the headings of Genre and Register.

The Register theory tells us *who* we are communicating with and our relationship with the person, *what* we are talking about and *how*—orally or in writing. Genre tells us how to organize what we will say for maximum impact. We will look at each theory in detail.

## Register

Every time we engage in a conversation, either written or oral, consciously or unconsciously, we vary the choice of words, structures and style that we use depending upon who we are making a conversation with. Sometimes even the language is chosen based on who we are making a conversation with. Derewianka (1990, p. 18) explained that the choices we make in a text depend on:

1. The relationship between the participants, that is the speaker/listener and the reader/writer. - tenor
2. The subject matter of the text. - field
3. The channel of communication—oral or written. - mode These three factors combine to determine the register of a text [Derewianka in (Angel M.Y. Lin, p. 15)]

Taking an example, when we write an official email to our superior, the language we use as well as the diction is much different from when we write an email to a colleague. Also, a comment on twitter is much different in its style, tone, and diction from a presentation we make in school. All of these are written communications, but their tenor and field are different.

'Register' in socio-linguistics has been defined by Halliday as "specific lexical and grammatical choices as made by speakers depending on the situational context, the participants of a conversation and the function of the language in the discourse" (cf. Halliday, 1989, p. 44).

Another explanatory definition for register is, "Language varies as its function varies; it differs in different situations. The label given to a variety of a language according to use is 'register'" (Chiu, 1973, p. 54).

Halliday identified 'Field', 'Tenor' and 'Mode' as the deciding factors for register. The register of a piece of communication depends on what the subject matter of the communication is, who the participants in the exchange are and how it is carried out. As mentioned earlier, we will only consider the written mode of communication in this book. Let us now analyse the manner in which field and tenor impact 'how' and 'what' we write or speak.

## Field Aspect of Register

What we communicate about has an impact on the language used to convey messages. Each topic has its jargon. To successfully engage with a subject and acquire the learning offered through it, it is imperative that the students understand subject related key terms and expressions whether as they listen to a teacher's lecture as she provides information on a topic, or as they partake of a discussion in the class on a subtopic connected to the subject or again, as they read concerned texts. The language chosen for interaction on varied subjects will change depending on the nature of the field, whether it is a specialized subject or a general one. Over the length of the teacher learning period, language used moves on from the simple, common, everyday articulation to specialized, technical, abstract and complex expression which is required for academic achievement.

## Tenor Aspect of Register

Who we communicate with, has a deep impact on the choice of words, grammar structures, style, tone and language used. If we are writing a project report being presented to a group of teachers for academic assessment, the student is likely to use precise language, specific terms, some subject specific specialized language and complex structures. The tone will be formal and expression succinct. There might be ideas to improve situations and suggestions for better effectiveness which will call for the use of abstract language too. On the contrary if a discussion with a friend is in process, there might still be specialized terms depending on the topic of discussion but the tone is likely to be informal and style, casual. Another facet of tenor is the role which the people in a communication are playing. This means that the same persons can engage in conversations in different capacities. A case in point is as follows. A student can engage with a teacher in the latter's capacity as a teacher and if the teacher is well-known as a friend to the student's parent/parents, then at another time as a family friend. Though the participants in the communication remain the same, their roles change and so does the tenor. This has an impact on the register of the exchange between them. The attitude within a communication changes with a change in roles of the communicators.

## Mode Aspect of Register

Mode refers to the output forms of language—oral or written. When we speak, we use a lot of fillers, facial expressions, gestures and at times even body postures. The additional speech features allow the listener to make meaning along with the language being used to convey a message. Another feature of the oral mode of communication is the free flow of ideas and thoughts. People speak and respond in a flow and there is little time to really think deep as a long pause before a response may result in a break in communication. In the written mode, however, all that there is the written word. Hence tools like signal words, a wide variety of adjectives to indicate degrees of emotions and adverbs to show an approximately exact action are required to make an expression as communicative as possible. There are no other features to help in a written communication.

Hence clarity of thought and expression along with precision are very important. These are ensured through the language and diction used to convey the message. Another aspect to consider is that written communication allows for more thought and reflection that might go into the communication. It permits the communicators to engage in a deeper connection, to understand what's being said, to identify gaps and fill them. As students move up in grades, they are expected to compose denser, more complex and abstract written texts wherein the language used is very different from the oral mode.

A close study of these three factors will help us predict the nature of the language students will need in different stages of their academic journey. This will be of much help in the teaching/ learning process that ensues through the academic expedition.

## Ahmar Mahboob's 3-Dimensional Model on Language Variation

Just as Halliday explains Register and its impact on language use through the elements of field, tenor, and mode, Ahmar Mahboob talks of the 'user', 'use' and 'mode'

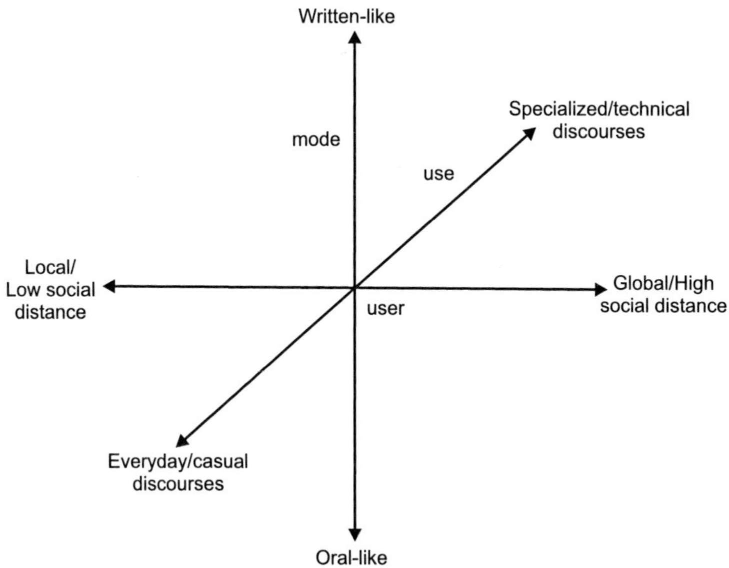


Mahboob's 3-Dimensional Model of Language Variation

Mode being the same, the 'user' refers to the people engaged in a communication and 'use' refers to the purpose of the communication. Mahboob arranges the 'users' of communication on a cline. At one end are our friends and family with whom we have a low social distance. We may also have a low social distance with people who share social factors like, age, nationality, gender, religion, profession, interests, etc. As we move on the cline towards the other end which is populated with language users with whom we have a high social distance, we place our neighbours, acquaintances, superiors, strangers, etc. The language we use to communicate with people on the low social distance point will be informal, perhaps verbose, replete with local jargon and even code switching. An interesting feature of the 'local language' is that users have a shared knowledge of the language and anyone not a part of the local group may not understand or relate to the terms and expressions used.

As we move towards the other end towards the people with high social distance, the language become more formal and impersonal. Communication with a person of high social distance will be specific, clear and to the point. The language has features making it ready for global understanding and the local elements are minimized.

The next dimension of language variation is 'use', that is, the purpose for which language is used. If the purpose is to make the other person comprehend a concept or theory, simple language might be used along with examples. If the purpose is discussion, the language used may have specialized terms and expressions and much reference to shared knowledge and understanding. This dimension draws a contrast between local everyday language and specialized discourse. An example here could be when a doctor addresses his/her patients and when s/he consults a fellow doctor on a case. In the former case the doctor is likely to use local and simple language while in the latter, specialized and complex as is demanded by the content of the discourse.

The final dimension of Mahboob's model is 'mode'. This dimension has been expressed as 'written like' on one end of the cline and 'oral like' on the other end. The addition of the word 'like' is indicative of the blurring lines between oral and written communication. With events like live chats, podcasts, internet calls, etc. the distinction has become weak. Quite a few modes of communication are either more written or more oral but not exclusively so.

Through his model, Ahmar Mahboob created eight domains between which language moves based on the dimensions discussed above.

| Domains | Situations in which the domain is active |
|---|---|
| Local Oral Everyday | Family members sharing their stories of the day and their experiences.<br>Language used is local and informal. Code switching between 2 or more shared languages is common. |
| Local Written Everyday | WhatsApp messaging, chats.<br>The language used is local and informal. Code switching between 2 or more shared languages may be used. |
| Local Oral Specialized | Colleagues who are also neighbours.<br>The language used may have workplace jargon and specialized terms and expressions specific to the shared field. For example, engineering, business, medicine, etc. |
| Local Written Specialized | WhatsApp group with colleagues and co-workers.<br>The language used may have workplace jargon and specialized terms and expressions specific to the shared field. For example, engineering, business, medicine, etc. |
| Global Oral Everyday | Meeting people in a lift or on a train who you do not know but strike a conversation to pass time.<br>Language used has minimal local content. The structures and simple and topics general. |
| Global Written Everyday | When we write 'To whomsoever it may concern' letters or when we write comments on blogs, etc.<br>Language is formal and to the point. Simple and clear to aid comprehension. |
| Global Oral Specialized | Presentation at symposiums or conferences.<br>The language used is specific to a field, is characterized by subject jargon and complex structures. The language used may not be comprehensible to someone not of the field. |
| Global Written Specialized | Research papers, journal articles, etc.<br>The language used is specific to a field, is characterized by subject jargon and complex structures. The language used may not be comprehensible to someone not of the field. |

These domains highlight the kind of language different situations need and demand. The kind of language mentioned in domains 1-4 is present in our environment at home and in the early years of school and we receive adequate exposure to them. The language required for domains 5 and 6 is one which we develop as our exposure to the world around us increases. It is the language required for communication in domains 7 and 8 that needs careful teaching. As we advance in our study, our education moves away from being generalized towards becoming specialized. As we start studying specialized fields of academics, the language we need to understand the subject matter and to express our knowledge thoughts and opinions on the varied topics of the subject matter, a need for the knowledge of Academic language arises. This Academic language must be systematically focused upon and taught. An effective way to impart an understanding of the specialized language required is to use contrastive analysis. Students compare local and global instances of language to identify areas of difference. They can then focus upon learning more about the unfamiliar domains of the latter language. They can be made aware of the characteristics that must be preferentially present and those that must be absent from global/Academic language.

In conclusion, I would like to say that understanding Register will be a motivating factor for the students as they will understand why they need to know and understand Academic language. Comprehension of Academic language will not only equip them for future educational ventures but also for the professional field of their choice which they are expected to join some years later. They will understand that to develop a sense of oneness with the professional fraternity they choose to belong with, they must learn to speak the shared language which is specialized. Thus, will begin their journey towards Academic language.

## Genre

An interesting way to think about genres is to think about how Netflix and Amazon categorize the movies and TV shows that they have for their audience.

Genre has been defined by many theorists and linguists. Some of the definitions are:

> A genre is defined as a category of text whose features have been identified and decided upon based on the intended audience, purpose, topic and mode of communication. (David Y.W. Lee, p. 38)
>
> "Genre" refers not only to types of literary texts but also to the predictable and recurring patterns of everyday, academic and literary texts occurring within a particular culture. (Hammond and Derewianka, 2001).
>
> Each genre is a formally identified and distinguishable variety of text that has achieved a level of general recognition whether in speech or writing.... A genre imposes several identifiable characteristics on a use of language, notably in relation to subject matter, purpose, textual structure, form of argumentation and level of formality.... (David Crystal, p. 210)
>
> Genre is a staged goal oriented, purposeful activity in which speakers engage as members of our culture. (Martin, 2001, p. 155)

In common parlance, genre is understood to be a particular type of text which has pre-decided characteristics. Each type of text is evaluated by the readers or listeners based on the absence or presence of these pre-defined features. For example, a joke, limerick, mystery, descriptive essay, etc. Each of these has pre-decided features which a reader will assess the text against when engaging with it. For instance, a horror story is expected to create goose bumps for a reader. If it does, it is labelled as a good read. In the same way, a joke is expected to have a comic element in it which will leave the reader or listener in splits.

It must also be acknowledged that genres have a social element. Genres emerged in response to the varied social purposes that communication was expected to achieve in a given culture. Different communities have different genres, e.g., the scientific community has laboratory reports, the business community has project feasibility reports, project development reports, the educational committee has student progress report, lesson plans and Course Descriptors. These are all different genres, and each has a layout, structure, language, register and purpose best known to members of the fraternity. These genres primarily, cater to the members of the community and are best understood by them too.

Some theorists like Swale (1990) have said that all those text types that serve the same purpose belong to the same genre. Taking this view forward Beverly Derewianka (1990) identified six genres based on the primary social purpose they fulfil. They are:

1. *Narratives*: They tell a story, usually to entertain. Some important and common features that we find in a narrative are a setting, characterization, a plot, a context, and a theme.
2. *Recount*: This is to tell what happened in the past. We find time references in a recount text and mostly a sequential movement.
3. *Information reports*: These provide factual information on a phenomenon or concept.
4. *Instruction*: This tells the listeners or readers what to do.
5. *Explanation*: To explain why or how a phenomenon happens. It might also provide information on what the impact of the phenomenon is.
6. *Expository texts*: These present or argue a viewpoint. Through this genre, issues are explored, and opinions arrived at based on evidence. While arguing a point of view, both for and against positions are explained at length and one position is taken based on valid justification and proof. (adapted from: Tuan Trong LUU. 122)

The language used within these texts, the organization of information, the linguistic structures, vocabulary, and expression, all correspond to the purpose each text is expected to achieve.

The following table presents the basic educational genres and their sub genres from Derewianka's "Trends and Issues in Genre-Based Approaches", p. 137.

While summing up, it is important to note that to realize its purpose, Genre needs register and language. If the register changes, it might change the genre and the associated language too. In fact, Martin (2001) says that Register and Genre are semiotic systems distinct from other semiotic systems such as language, music, etc. in the sense that they both are kinds of parasites that have no structure of their own. To gain significance, they have to make use of the instrument of language.

## Conclusion

Having looked at the most important elements that define Academic language, it is assumed that the reader would have developed a fair understanding of Academic language. It is the need of this new educational attitude that all academic understanding must be expressed in specialized Academic language, the language that we seldom encounter in our day to day communicative ventures, the language that is found only in the highly exclusive areas in school and in other related pedagogical contexts. As identified, the key to acquiring and learning Academic language is a deep and real understanding of genre and register and how they impact the choice of language and diction.

Academic language, in general, has some features peculiar to it. These we will study in the next chapter.

## Works Cited

Ahmar Mahboob. *Summit on the Future of TESOL PROFESSION*, Tesol International Association, 2017, www.academia.edu/34196843/Reimagining_Language_Competence_On_professionalism.

Derewianka, Beverly. "Trends and Issues in Genre-Based Approaches." *RELC Journal*, vol. 34, no. 2, 2003, pp. 133-54, doi: 10.1177/003368820303400202.

Derewianka, Beverly. "Teaching Writing in Today's Classrooms: Looking Back to Looking Forward." *Teaching Writing in Today's Classrooms: Looking Back to Look Forward*, edited by Jan Turbill et al., Australian Literary Educators' Association, 2015, pp. 69-86.

Engberg, Jan, et al. *Reflections upon Genre: Encounters between Literature, Knowledge and Emerging Communicative Conventions*. Narr, 2014, www.researchgate.net/publication/264160574_Reflections_upon_

genre_encounters_between_literature_knowledge_and_emerging_communicative_conventions.

"Genres: Linguistic or Social Practices." *Discourse and Genre: Using Language in Context*, by Stephen Bax, Palgrave Macmillan, 2011, p. 47.

Gottlieb, Margo H., and Gisela Ernst-Slavit. *Academic Language in Diverse Classrooms: Mathematics, Grades 3-5: Promoting Content and Language Learning*. Corwin, 2013.

Halliday, Michael A.K. "Linguistics and Education." *Linguistics and Education*, 1993, doi.org/10.1016/0898-5898(93)90026-7.

Jarkach-Azdoud, Hicham, and David Crystal. "A Dictionary of Linguistics & Phonetics David Crystal." *Academia.edu*, 2008, www.academia.edu/23349059/A_Dictionary_of_Linguistics_and_Phonetics_David_Crystal.

Lee, David Y.V. "Genres, Registers, Text Types, Domains and Styles: Clarifying the Concepts and Navigating a Path through the BNC Jungle." *Language Learning & Technology*, vol. 5, no. 3, Sept. 2001, doi: http://llt.msu.edu/vol5num3/lee/.

Lukin, Annabelle, et al. "Halliday's Model of Register Revisited and Explored." *Linguistics and Human Sciences*, vol. 4, no. 2, 2011, pp. 187-213, doi: 10.1558/lhs.v4i2.187.

Luu, Trong Tuan. "Teaching Writing through Genre-Based Approach." https://www.researchgate.net, Academy Publication, Nov. 2011, www.oalib.com/paper/2272761.

Rose, David. "Genre in the Sydney School." Edited by James Paul Gee and Michael Handford, *Academia.edu*, Routledge, London, 2010, www.academia.edu/36763275/Routledge_Handbook_of_Discourse_Analysis.

Rose, David. "Analysing Pedagogic Discourse: An Approach from Genre and Register." *Functional Linguistics*, SpringerOpen, 31 Dec. 2014, functionallinguistics.springeropen.com/articles/10.1186/ s40554-014-0011-4.

Zwiers, Jeff. *Building Academic Language: Essential Practices for Content Classrooms 5-12*. Jossey-Bass, 2008.

# 3
# The Essentials of Academic Writing

After an elaborate analysis of Academic language, let us now shift our attention to Academic Writing, which is the primary concern of this work. It is important to note that the language used for Academic writing is distinctly different from the language we use for informal writing like that found in friendly notes, WhatsApp messages, letters to friends, online chats, etc. While this informal communication is characterised by slangs (*kudos, bottom line*), colloquial language (*really...like really?*), distorted grammar (*me too coming*) with sound spellings (*wud, cud, dunno*), simplicity of expression and sometimes even verbosity, the hallmark of Academic writing is its specificity, complete absence of slangs, accuracy and complexity of expression, objective articulation and formal style and register. It is important to identify and delineate the attributes and essential functions of Academic writing, for an effective assimilation of the same in the teaching and learning process. The primary reason for the invention of language was communication between man and man. In due course of time language was used to record events, to learn about things, to make contracts and present information to both a known and an unknown audience. With further progress and identification of particularized communication needs, different kinds of languages with well-defined features and functions were recognized. Academic language was one such tributary of language that came into existence. Some of the common objectives outlined for Academic language were comparing and contrasting, exemplifying, classifying, interpreting, presenting inferencing, hypothesizing, defining, predicting, expressing cause and effect relationships as well as opinions.

Apart from there being specific language requirements for each of the above-mentioned functions, there are also organizational requirements related to each, though, there may be some overlapping.

Now that we are aware of some of the functions that Academic language is used to perform, let us look at some important features of Academic writing. They are:

1. Presentation of voice
2. Formality of style and register
3. Use of hedging in articulation
4. Grammar in Academic writing

### 1. Presentation of Voice

A common purpose in Academic writing while analysing, evaluating or responding to a pronouncement is to make a point/ claim and support it with credible evidence of prior research, logical reasoning and appropriate examples. While the claims and points are those of the writer, contributions of previous researchers and theorists can be used to support the same.

'Voice' in Academic writing refers to the varied voices that we hear in a written piece. These voices are mainly that of the writer and those of the contributors who have researched on the topic of discussion in the writing and whose works have been cited by the author to support his claim, point or observation. These contributors are eminent and acclaimed thinkers in the field to which the written text being referred to relates. Though the presence of both the voices is indispensable, yet it is critical to identify the order of their importance. It is of prime significance to understand here that the voice of the writer, even if he/she is not yet a recognized author, is the most important and care should be taken that this voice does not get lost in the maze of the voices of the other contributors. It must be remembered at all times that the most important voice in a piece of Academic writing is that of the author which is only being supported by the voices of the contributors.

When a piece is written for an audience, what the latter wants is to know what the writer thinks about a claim or point based on his or her own research and comprehension of the varied reading expectedly undertaken. The reader is interested in knowing what led the author to believe what he states in his write up. In the process of explaining the thought route to the audience, the writer can cite previous works of seminal researchers and pioneers in the field indeed. However, the academic piece should not appear to be a collection of quotes on the topic from accomplished and influential names rather than an original take on something. Care and caution should be exercised to ensure that an academic piece comes across as an expression of a personal and singular opinion and thought rather than as a compilation of citations.

The most important reason why an author might call upon experienced voices in support of his or her claim is lack of confidence and conviction in the soundness of a novice though possibly novel observation or idea. It is commonly felt that by frequently referring to established and accepted works, the audience will be more inclined to accept the argument and will award recognition more easily and readily. It is important to mention here that in the dynamic academic world, a fresh and new notion, presented in a logical flow with a well-explained conception process and supported by valid explanations and linked contributions from prominent thinkers in the field is more than welcome.

There are two ways to weave in a contributor's voice in a piece of researched writing other than through quotes. One is paraphrasing and the other is summarizing. Paraphrasing involves rewriting someone else's thoughts in the words, expression and style of the writer himself or herself. The paraphrase is a reflection of the understanding of the writer of the contributor's essential ideas and information expressed in a unique diction and style. At times, a paraphrase also serves the purpose of clarifying a point or simplifying it. Paraphrasing is also used in place of a quote to maintain the consistency in style or to avoid lengthy quotations which in the original form may not appear to support the claim. However, it is important to maintain the precision of the message that has been paraphrased. Look at the example below.

> **Original**
>
> Despite the undoubted fact that everyone's vision of what constitutes success is different, one should spend one's time establishing and finalizing one's personal vision of it. Otherwise, how can you possibly understand what your final destination might be, or whether or not your decisions are assisting you in moving in the direction of the goals which you've set yourself?
>
> The two kinds of statements—mission and vision—can be invaluable to your approach, aiding you, as they do, in focusing on your primary goal, and quickly identifying possibilities that you might wish to exploit and explore.
>
> **Paraphrase**
>
> We all have different ideas about success. What's important is that you spend time defining your version of success. That way, you'll understand what you should be working toward. You'll also know if your decisions are helping you to move toward your goals.
>
> Used as part of your personal approach to goal setting, mission and vision statements are useful for bringing sharp focus to your most important goal, and for helping you to quickly identify which opportunities you should pursue.
>
> (*example taken from* https://www.mindtools.com)

Summarizing is essentially an overview of an entire discussion or argument. It involves identifying the main points that encase the essence of a part of a text or an entire text and presenting them in a condensed form. A summary is much shorter than the original content. Summarizing is resorted to when the writer wants to highlight the key points in a work of research to corroborate a claim or to make comprehension of an idea easier. The following example will illustrate the point.

**Original**

So how do you go about identifying your strengths and weaknesses, and analyzing the opportunities and threats that flow from them? SWOT Analysis is a useful technique that helps you to do this.

What makes SWOT especially powerful is that, with a little thought, it can help you uncover opportunities that you would not otherwise have spotted. And by understanding your weaknesses, you can manage and eliminate threats that might otherwise hurt your ability to move forward in your role.

If you look at yourself using the SWOT framework, you can start to separate yourself from your peers, and further develop the specialized talents and abilities that you need in order to advance your career and to help you achieve your personal goals.

**Summary**

SWOT analysis is a technique that helps you identify strengths, weakness, opportunities, and threats. Understanding and managing these factors helps you to develop the abilities you need to achieve your goals and progress in your career.

(*example taken from* https://www.mindtools.com)

In both the cases cited, it is imperative to give credit to the original thinker or researcher. Both tools are used when the message in a text is more important than the original communication. They also save time and space in an academic write up.

Another aspect of 'voice' that must be brought to the notice of the readers is the use of active and passive voice in Academic writing. An expression is called passive when the person, thing, event, etc. who receives an action becomes more important than the doer of the action. In contrast, an active expression is used when the doer of an action is identified and is the focus of attention. The use of an active or a passive voice depends on the purpose of a piece of writing. If the purpose is to make the readers notice events and happenings rather than what or who caused the same, the use of passive is more likely. On the contrary if the perpetrator of an action or happening is important and must be highlighted, the use of active voice is recommended. For example, in history the achievements of various kings and emperors is important. It is important for us to know that Shah Jahan built the Taj Mahal. That the Taj Mahal was built is of significance however to know that it was built by Emperor Shah Jahan is equally important. It is imperative to note, that the active and passive, both give the same information but from two different perspectives. Going back to the example above, when we say "the Taj Mahal was built by Shah Jahan", we learn something about the Taj Mahal, while when we say, "Shah Jahan built the Taj Mahal", we learn something about Shah Jahan.

Essentially, the choice of using the passive or active voice depends on more factors other than the message which the writer wants to convey and the aspect which s/he wants to stress upon. The choice of voice also depends on the discipline being represented for and the conventions of that discipline. For example, in the early twentieth century scientists preferred to use passive forms in writing papers in Science for its impersonal expression. However, in the 1929, with the introduction of the APA style (American Psychological Association), preference for the active form became prevalent when the APA style document stated "Verbs are vigorous, direct communicators. Use the active rather than the passive voice, and select tense or mood carefully." Researchers feel that while passive forms make a writing verbose and circumlocutory, active verbs make the same clear and concise. Though in Academic writing the thrust is on impersonal expression but researchers in the field of Science feel that the writer or researcher's action and presence should be felt in an acknowledged piece.

In any composition, the choice of active or passive voice depends on the discretion of the writer who is primarily driven by some considerations and requirements. One such consideration is when the writer wants to focus on the receiver of an action and not on the doer. In this case the passive voice is an appropriate choice and is very useful in highlighting the important aspects, participants, or events by placing them right at the beginning of a sentence. For example, "Glass has been classified as a solid." Another instance in which you can adopt the passive style of writing is to avoid the use of personal pronouns to make a writing impersonal or objective and hence formal. Yet another reason to adopt the passive style is when it is unnecessary to mention the doer or when it is obvious who the doer is. For example, "Each feature of Academic writing has been discussed in detail." Here it is understood that the author has discussed the features at length. We do not need to say, "the writer has discussed each feature of...." Sometimes, the writer may not know who the doer is. For example, "The Lund Cathedral was built in the 12th century." Here the writer cannot use the active voice as no one is sure who really built it. A writer may deliberately choose to use the passive form when s/he does not purposely reveal who the doer is. The author may want to conceal the doer for several reasons ranging from personal to public interest. Using the passive voice in this case is a beautiful way of putting forth useful information without being dishonest.

## 2. Formality of Style and Register

Another characteristic feature of Academic writing is its formal style and register. Formality of a piece of writing is determined on the basis of its tone, choice of words and how those words are strung together to make meaning. The primary purpose of a formal piece of writing is to communicate ideas, thoughts or information of high importance in a clear, concise and precise manner to an audience that is socially distant and, in many cases, unknown. A socially distant audience connotes that the writer and the audience are aware of each other in a professional capacity or in an academic context but are not familiar with each other in their social surroundings. A social distance also means that the writer and the audience may not be sharing a common social or economic setting. This explains the rule stating that formal communication must not use clichés and colloquial expressions. Some more important rules that define formal writing are as follows:

- Sentences in formal writing should be complete, complex and should add specific meaning to the communication.
- The vocabulary used should be relevant to the field of reference and the usage should be commonly acceptable.
- Standard spelling and punctuation should be used.
- Appropriate referencing norms should be followed.
- The writing should reflect coherence of thought and cohesion of expression.
- Sentences should not start with coordinating conjunctions like 'so', 'and', 'but' or 'because'. They should rather start with an appropriate transition words like however, although, additionally, etc.

Essentially, in professional or Academic writing, the writer is expected to pack in maximum meaning in as succinct an expression as possible. It is because of this reason that formal writing assumes a considerable degree of complexity.

The choice of expression and words in a writing also expresses an author's tone or attitude towards the topic of discussion. The tone in Academic writing is expected to be neutral or unbiased and objective. The claims made by the writer should be backed by adequate research and relevant evidence cited in support. The writer's claims and understanding should be appropriately substantiated by the reasons for the belief with a clear reference to material that was studied to reach the stated conclusion. This path lends a formal tone to a piece of Academic writing.

Register is another aspect of Academic writing without which a consideration of the feature of style is incomplete. In fact, at this point, it is significant to draw a contrast between 'Style' and 'Register'. In writing, the choice of words and expressions are primarily decided by the 'register' of a communication situation. The 'register' of a communication situation is based on what the topic of discussion is and the purpose of the discussion. For instance, two medical practitioners are likely to use the register of medicine when communicating for the purpose of a case deliberation while the same two people when arguing to decide who the current best Tennis player is, might use the register associated with the particular sport. Hence, the register changes with the purpose and topic of a speech situation. On the other hand, the style of writing a piece of communication depends on the relationship between the people who are engaged in the communication and the venue where the communication is taking place. For instance, a conversation between two friends or relatives has an informal style while that between a lawyer and a judge will be formal in style. However, if the lawyer and the judge meet in an informal situation, say a cinema hall, the conversation may have a lower level of formality. Style and register are connected in many ways. Drawing from the example above, the lawyer is expected to use the legal parlance if the dialogue is about a case in the court. However, if the talk is about the latest movie that has been released, the register will change though the style may continue to be formal.

In Academic writing, the style is always formal since the audience is always considered to be socially distant, although the register keeps changing, depending on the topic of the research paper, article, essay, information piece, etc.

### 3. Use of Hedging in Articulation

Academic research is about stating facts and talking about their perceived implications. Whether it is the sciences or the arts, researchers study and re-study facts and make claims based on their understanding and percipience. Though these claims may be supported by valid explanations and evidences, they are often challenged by contemporary or future academicians. To protect themselves from an academic 'attack', writers usually use 'vague language' or 'hedging'. Hedging is an art in writing whereby the writer deliberately uses non-committal or ambiguous expression while making a claim through building probability into the articulation of claims. It is the writer's attempt to be confidently uncertain while making an academic assertion.

Apart from safeguarding against direct opposition from fellow researchers, other reasons to use hedging may be to follow the norm established in the given specific style of writing and to politely accept that no research is flawless by acknowledging that there can be a limitation in the proposed theory. The writer wants to come across as one receptive of varying views and not someone who believes that s/he knows it all. At this juncture it must be emphasized that being uncertain does not mean a confused state of mind. In fact, in some cases a writer may wish to blunt the edge of his research findings because their evidence is not so strongly conclusive.

- Hedging can be achieved through various ways. Writers might use any of the following ways to hedge their claims:
- Use modals like 'can', 'could', 'might', etc. For instance, 'this combination of chemicals might lead to a strong explosion.'
- Probability adjectives like 'probable', 'likely' or 'possible'. For example, 'such neglect from parents is likely to cause personality disorders in the children.'
- Adverbs like 'perhaps', 'practically', etc. For example, 'the theory is practically invalid in this case.'
- Nouns like 'assumption', 'claim', 'virtually' can also be used.

Hedging is a common practice in Academic writing. It is a cautious and polite approach to stating claims and making way for more research initiatives on a topic. The opposite of hedging is boosting. Boosters are lexical devices used to express conviction and can be used to propel a claim into notice. Use of expressions like 'really', 'absolutely', 'obviously', etc. make the reader believe that the writer is convinced of his research findings or claims. However, few writers in academics use boosters. It is mostly hedgers that are more common.

### 4. Grammar in Academic Writing

Academic writing is characterized by accurate grammar and complex expression. Both of these require that the writer be aware of the relevant grammar concepts such as nominalization, complex sentence formation which includes knowledge of the varied clauses, primarily, relative clause which in turn helps to clarify references thereby resolving confusions of who did what. Another grammar aspect that needs serious attention is punctuation. The way a writer punctuates his written communication can make or break the message being conveyed. Transition expressions of linking markers are another important aspect that need to be covered. Let us look at some of the grammar concepts mentioned here.

### A. Nominalization

Nominalization is an important feature of Academic writing. It allows the writer to be objective and impersonal as well as pack in relevant information into the writing. Another major achievement is that the focus of the reader is directed towards the object, event, or concept rather than on the doer. Nominalization also allows more information being put together in a sentence concisely. As a result, the write up is more abstract, formal, and dense which is exactly what is required. As per Thompson (2004) and Eggins (1994), one important function of nominalization is condensation. Elma Kerz in her article "The Cognitive and Pragmatic Motivations for the use of Nominalizations in Academic writing", quotes Martin and talks about the role of nominalization.

> .... Nominalizations allow the author to generalize about processes without specifying the precise circumstances and the conditions under which the research was carried out. This in turn is related to the passive aspect of nominalization, viz., to make arguments sound and 'not accessible to debate'. (Martin, 1985)

Nominalization, additionally, allows for a holistic viewing of the research process. The objectivity and impersonality of the writing style introduced in a piece of writing through nominalization is a recognized and desirable feature of Academic writing. Authors of academic texts prefer to identify the role of the human agency in knowledge construction only passively.

The term 'nominalization' was first coined by John Williams in his book, *Style: Towards Clarity and Grace*. To define nominalization formally, it is a process through which verbs and adjectives are changed to their noun forms with or without morphological modification and used as the head of a noun phrase.

> An illustration of nominalization is given below—"We analyzed the results of the survey." (normal sentence)
>
> "The results of the survey were analyzed." (nominalized sentence)

If we notice, the doer of the analysis has been obscured and the event of the analysis has been moved to the forefront so that the reader focus on the event rather than on the doer.

There are two ways of achieving nominalization. One is by changing verbs and adjectives to their noun form. Verbs can be converted to nouns by adding '-tion', '-ity', '-ness', '-ment', '-ship', etc. Another way to achieve the same result as this is to use verbs as nouns and add a 'to' before it. For instance, 'to show', 'to raise', etc. Adjectives can be changed to nouns by adding suffixes like '-ism', '-ity' and '-ness'.

A noteworthy reason why authors adopt nominalization is their desire for objectivity in their writing. Researchers want their claims to be seen as a result of exploration and analysis not as their personal perspective and belief. Douglas Biber and Bethany Grey in their article, "Nominalizing the Verb Phrase in Academic Science Writing", refer to Halliday's "Grammatical Metaphor" as being strongly related to the concept of nominalization. Halliday explains this theory of "Grammatical Metaphors" as a situation in which nouns are used to convey meanings beyond their designated category. Traditionally, nouns refer to entities; however, nominalization is a process through which nouns are used to refer to processes, events, and qualities though this is actually the task of verbs and adjectives.

It is relevant here to bring in Helen Sword's perspective. She decries nominalization as an action that kills the spirit of a writing and makes it lifeless. It unnecessarily complicates expression and defeats the purpose of a write up which is a clear communication with the reader. Despite this perspective, corpus investigations by Biber and Gray (2016) have revealed that the use of nominal/phrasal structures over verb phrases has increased in specialized Academic writing in all academic registers. However, this change has had little impact on the non-informational and fictional writing like prose and drama. This movement towards nominalization has primarily been observed in highly specialized writing meant for a specialized audience. Though today nominalization has pervaded in all streams, Halliday and Webster (2009) argue that nominalization in all probability developed first in scientific and technical genres and then gradually extended and spread to other realms of academic written expression assuming indispensability in any impactful or powerful piece of writing.

### *B. Clauses*

Academic writing is loaded with composite thoughts, ideas, opinions and claims which require the use of complex expression. Complex expression leads us to the use of clauses in writing. Knowledge of the various kinds of clauses and how they combine to present multiple ideas is imperative for a researcher and an academician as the stated information allows the authors to incorporate abstraction, depth, and density into their work.

It is mandatory for an informational writer to be aware of the various kind of clauses like independent clauses, dependent clauses, relative clauses, complement clauses, adjectival clauses, and adverbial clauses to name the more important ones. Accurate and appropriate use of clauses can be a wonderful tool in the hands of an author to pack in and present useful information in complex yet compact packets. In fact, whenever it is critical to develop ideas to show logical connections, writers often resort to a combination of clauses to develop a concise, direct and well-structured argument.

Douglas Biber and Bethany Gray (pp. 92-99) in a research they conducted on the use of the varied clauses state in their paper that dependent clauses functioning as constituents of noun phrases are preferred in Academic writing. Their research results further state that noun complement clauses (*that* and *to*), WH and non-finite relative clauses are also quite commonly used in this genre of writing.

To conclude, the vital role of clauses in lending complexity, abstraction, conciseness, and density to writing for academic purposes in varied forms can never be underestimated.

### *C. Punctuation*

Punctuation is another aspect of Academic writing that can never be overstated. It is a feature that might make or break the message being conveyed in a written piece. To highlight the importance of punctuation in writing, the *Penguin Guide to Punctuation* rightly says that while speaking English we have a host of tools at our disposal which help us to accurately and appropriately convey an intended message to the listeners. Some of these paralinguistic tools are intonation, pitch, tone, style, stress, rhythm, pauses as well as, the possibility of calling for a repetition from the speaker. In writing, however, we just have punctuation at our disposal to fulfil all the responsibilities required to convey the message accurately and appropriately to the reader. To recognize and support the role that punctuation has to fulfil, a standard system has been put in place. This system is consistent and lays out the function associated with each punctuation mark clearly. Hence every mark of punctuation has a well-defined job profile with a clearly designated role and responsibilities. An academician is expected to be aware of this standard system and use it appropriately as and where required so that the communication endeavoured through a written piece is successfully completed.

Though each punctuation mark has its importance, in academic expression the ‘full stop’ or the ‘period’ and the ‘comma’ are of paramount significance. While the ‘period’ marks the end of an idea or a thought, a ‘comma’ is a mid-sentence punctuation which segregates dependent and independent clauses and phrases to help the reader make appropriate meaning. Apart from marking the end of a thought or idea, there are some more important uses or functions of the period(.). It is used to indicate that the abbreviated form of a word has been used. For example, we write e.g. for ‘for instance’, etc. for ‘et cetera’. We also use the period to show that some part of a text has been left out. In this case we use three dots in a row. This symbol is called an ‘ellipsis’. This is a tool normally used when quoting long texts from other research works. One can write the first few words of the text to show the start point and the last few to mark the end point. One could also include the important points in the text, the ones which require to be brought to the notice of the reader in support of a claim or point. Look at the illustration below,

-The complete quote-

> "The forest fire was raging. While trees were being burnt down and animal engulfed in the blaze, humans were setting up committees to determine the cause of the fire rather than taking steps to contain the same before it brought down the entire forest."

-The same quote with ellipsis-

> "The forest fire was raging. While trees were being burnt down...rather than taking steps to contain the same before it brought down the entire forest."

Here the 'ellipsis' has been used to remove the middle part of a quote from a survey report.

Another punctuation symbol which is much faultily used is the 'comma'. This could be because of the variety of ways in which the 'comma' can be used and consequently may cause confusion. The technicalities involved in the use of the 'comma' can be bewildering. The main use of this punctuation mark in Academic writing is to separate the subordinate clauses from the main clause. Let us look at some of the various functions of the 'comma':

- To separate the transition or adverbial phrase at the beginning of a sentence from the main clause. For example, 'However,...', 'as a result,....', 'After the meeting was over,...' etc.
- To segregate the main clause from the subordinate clauses which are an indispensable part of complex sentence structure which is a preferential attribute of Academic writing. The purpose of using the comma like this is to indicate to the reader the information which is central and that which is not so essential. The subordinate clause can be at the beginning or in the middle of a complete sentence. At the beginning it will require only one comma while in the middle it

will require two commas, one at the beginning of the clause and one at the end of the clause.

- To separate the items in a list.
- To introduce an interjection, that is, to introduce a break in thought or to add an extra detail.

Having discussed the uses of the 'comma' in Academic writing, let us now look at the errors that writers make while using this punctuation mark. Some of the errors are adding an extra comma in a sentence either between a verb and its object, between a main clause and its dependent clause or between coordination clauses separated by conjunctions. These can lead to derivations of meanings which were never intended. Mostly authors end up placing extra commas in their sentences to reflect a break in their thought or the need for a pause. This leads to many mistakes in formal writing.

For example, one should never believe in what one reads without considering its source.

Here the author perceives a break after never and expresses the pause with a comma which is not really required.

Another error common in the use of the 'comma' is 'the comma splice'. A splice occurs when two independent clauses are separated by a comma instead of the appropriate punctuation or conjunction. Most of the times this mistake happens when the authors write in the style they speak. For example:

> "The local residents were not happy with the compensation they received for their lands from the government, nobody looked into this issue and the construction of the complex started."

The above is an illustration of the comma splice as the two independent clauses have been erroneously separated by a comma. This can be corrected by placing a *semicolon* in place of the comma or by introducing the conjunction '*but*'. Look at the examples as given below.

> "The local residents were not happy with the compensation they received for their lands from the **government; nobody** looked into this issue and the construction of the complex started."

> "The local residents were not happy with the compensation they received for their lands from the government **but** nobody looked into this issue and the construction of the complex started."

Yet another mistake which authors make in the use of the comma is to miss placing a comma where needed. This often happens when the writer is not very confident in using the comma and is scared that he or she may use it incorrectly. Hence it is missed at places where it should have been. This can often lead to unintended and ambiguous meaning. The absence of appropriate commas makes a text difficult to read and cause stress to the reader. For instance,

> "The application can scan print save send and edit documents."

> "However, the results were not indicative of the downward journey that had been predicted."

The semicolon and the colon are also useful punctuation marks. The semicolon is used to link two independent clauses which are connected. For example,

> "The research was conducted; a report was made and presented to the partners."

An error takes place when the writer puts two unconnected independent clauses together and links them with a semicolon.

> "It was cold as predicted; the MET department had advised against stepping out of the house unless absolutely necessary to avoid medical issues."

> "It was cold as predicted; we decided to hold the survey at a later date."

In both the above examples, the latter clauses are not really related to the former ones since holding a survey is not decidedly based on weather conditions at most times. It would hence be inappropriate to link the two sentences by a semicolon. Having discussed the semicolon, let us move on to talking about the colon which is used at the end of an independent clause to add more information about the independent clause, that is, add an explanation, emphasis or elaboration on the idea expressed in the independent clause. In this aspect, the colon and the semicolon are different. While the semicolon places the sentences it links on an equal footing, the colon emphasizes or highlights the second clause more than the first one.

Another punctuation mark which holds much importance is the quotation mark, single, and double. As per tradition, the single quotation marks are used to place quotes within quotes, and the quotes should be placed outside the period at the end. A critical point to note here is that in Academic writing, quotation marks are not meant to be used to push individual words into ordinary focus.

The above are the punctuation symbols that are frequently used in Academic writing and a knowledge of their use stands a writer in good stead.

### *D. Linking Markers*

Linking markers, linking words, transitions, discourse markers are all names of a very special glue that binds the thoughts and ideas expressed in a piece of Academic writing together. Their inclusion in articulation lends depth and maturity to a text. They are like signboards on the road which guide a traveller towards his or her destination efficiently and effectively. They support the reader to traverse through a written piece gaining comprehension and making meaning of the text.

Linking markers are expressions like 'although', 'however', 'additionally', 'as a result', 'another example of', etc. which are used to indicate the relationship between two thoughts or ideas in a complex expression. These markers have defined functions like reinforcing an idea through an additional example, providing more information on a particular topic, presenting a contrasting idea, conceding to an idea, etc. They appear at the initial position in a sentence or clause while some others appear in the middle, between two clauses. They are almost always followed by a comma. For instance,

> "Although, the results for the competition were delayed they were announced well before the party broke up."

> "Jones's ideas about how the crime was committed are creative and interesting, although, they did not take into account the fact that two of the four people being implicated with this act were behind bars at the time of the crime."

A short indicative list of some of the linking markers is given below.

| Function | Linking expressions | Position in a sentence/ clause |
|---|---|---|
| Adding information | Moreover; in addition; additionally; further; further to this; also; besides; what is more. | Initial Position |
| Presenting a contrast | However; on the other hand; in contrast; yet. | Initial Position |
| Indicating an example | For example; for instance; to illustrate; to show | Initial Position |
| Indicating the result of something | Therefore; consequently; in consequence; as a result; accordingly; hence; thus; for this reason; because of this. | Initial Position |
| Emphasizing a point | As a matter of fact; in fact; indeed; above all | Initial Position |
| Stating reasons | Because; since; as; in so far as. | Initial Position |
| Expressing a condition | If; in the event of; as long as...; so long as...; provided that...; assuming that...; given that.... | Initial Position |
| Expressing a comparison | as well as; in comparison; identically; similarly; unlike; parallel to | Initial Position |
| Expressing a conclusion or summation | finally, to conclude; to end; to recapitulate; in short; to summarize | |
| To express a generalization | generally, essentially, in essence; largely; primarily; broadly speaking | |

Discourse markers help connect ideas within a paragraph by establishing a logical link between the point or claim expressed and the explanations and elaboration provided, and examples given in support of the point or claim. They also serve to establish a link between two paragraphs and lend cohesiveness to an entire essay. So effectively they play a dual role. The expressions are the same although their role expands.

It is critical to note at this point that care should be taken to balance the use of discourse markers when writing an Academic text. While the absence or presence of very few linkers in a text may make it appear illogically constructed and the connections between ideas abstruse, an over use of discourse markers may make a text appear artificial and unnecessarily complicated and heavy to the reader. It must be kept in mind that the main role of the linking markers is to make a text cohesive and reader-friendly for the audience and help them move through the text with ease while making meaning of and connecting with what they read. Hence the transitions should be used only when and where required.

## Conclusion

The main impetus behind this discussion on the features of Academic writing was to highlight the areas of language and grammar that a person wanting to learn the craft must master. Deep and accurate knowledge of each of the areas delineated namely, voice, style, register, grammar as well as hedging is essential to being able to write essays, research papers or any other texts of academic context.

## Works Cited

Aarts, Bas, et al. "Nominalizing the Verb Phrase in Academic Science Writing." *Verb Phrase in English: Investigating Recent Language Change with Corpora*, Cambridge University Press, 2013, pp. 99-132.

Biber, Douglas, and Bethany Gray. *Grammatical Complexity in Academic English: Linguistic Change in Writing*. Cambridge University Press, 2016.

Burgess, Sally, et al. "The Cognitive and Pragmatic Motivations for the Use of Nominalizations in Academic Texts." *English as an Additional Language in Research Publication and Communication*, Verlag Peter Lang, 2008, pp. 123-38.

Eggins, Suzanne. *Language as Context: Introduction to Systemic Functional Linguistics*. Pinter Publishers, 1994.

Halliday, M.A.K., and Jonathan J. Webster. *Linguistic Studies of Text and Discourse*. Continuum, 2002.

Halliday, M.A.K., and Jonathan Webster. *On Language and Linguistics*. Continuum International Publishing, 2003.

Jalilifar, Alireza, et al. "Exploring Nominalization in Scientific Textbooks: A Cross-Disciplinary Study of Hard and Soft Sciences." *International Journal of English Studies*, vol. 17, no. 2, 2017, p. 1, doi:10.6018/ijes/2017/2/272781.

Patt, Sebastian. "Punctuation as a means of medium-dependent presentation structure in English - el libro t." *El libro tcnico*, narr francke attempto VERLAG, www.ellibrotecnico.com/ebook/punctuationas-a-means-of-medium-dependent-presentation-structure-in-english_E1000648714.

Simon-Vandenbergen, A.M. "Grammatical Metaphor: Views from Systemic Functional Linguistics." *Google Books*, John Benjamins Publishing, 1 Jan. 2003, books.google.com/books/about/Grammatical_Metaphor.html?id=mQHfh1OShqEC.

Sword, Helen. *Stylish Academic Writing*. Harvard University Press, 2012.

# 4

# Organization of Content in Academic Texts

The importance of organization is undeniable, be it in any aspect of our lives. This importance arises from the purpose that it fulfils which is to make things promptly and easily accessible as well as save time and energy. The same principle is applicable to the field of Academic writing where content is organized within a given framework to help the reader effectively engage himself/ herself with the message being communicated rather than expend energy on trying to make sense of what is written and how it is logically connected. Research says that 55% readers will read an article for 15 seconds to decide whether they want to read on or not. Efficient organization allows a quick scan to reveal whether the article is relevant or not and this quality makes it an important factor which helps people decide further in favour or against engagement with a write up. Along with a good general layout, appropriate headings and linking phrases are also keys to an effective layout.

When two people communicate, the language used and the flow of exchange depends on the level of familiarity shared between the two participants of the communication. For instance, a teacher may have well established the use of shorthand in class for some of the concepts or rules which are shared knowledge between the teacher and the students. When the teacher uses these shorthand symbols in class, there is no difficulty in comprehension at all on the part of the students who have complete understanding of the shorthand codes. However, to any outsider the use of codes might appear to be an impediment in communication for lack of a common language pool. In Academic writing scenarios, the communication is between roles rather than between people hence the scope of misunderstanding is high considering that the familiarity level between the two roles may be zero. In order to make up for a lack of this familiarity we have standardized structures for presentation of academic information which both writers as well as readers recognize. This makes the knowledge of structure almost indispensable. The most important purpose of a piece of Academic writing is to reach out to its target audience. For achieving this goal, the writer tries to fathom the reader's expectation from the text and lays out information in a manner that to his or her mind will engage the latter effectively.

Having deciphered the reason for the prime importance of organization in Academic Writing, let us now look at the types of writing that students are required to produce. In school and college students primarily compose what I have chosen to call, *Response essays* and *Research essays*. *Response essays* are essays like argumentative essays, compare and contrast essay, descriptive essays and the like which may present a perspective, justify, defy or interpret to create new knowledge concerned with an existing piece of data to create new wisdom. The research involved is only to gather support for a claim made in the context of the said knowledge. There are no gaps identified in the prevailing information. Rather the existing information is twisted around to create a new understanding of the same. On the contrary, *Research Articles/essays* seek to introduce a piece of data which may not have existed before or had existed but not in the same strain as researched by the academician. These essays call for experimentation with elements or observation of the same as they either cause or react to manipulation to reveal a new learning. Such write ups are called upon mostly at the higher education level as they place a high demand on the mental faculties and the need of a mature approach which comes only after a certain level of academic exposure and brain development.

An essay, for optimum comprehensibility, must be planned and organized at three levels and appeal to the readers. These are the *macro*, *meso* and the *micro* levels. The *macro* level is concerned with the overall presentation of the essay and to the inclusion of an introduction, some body paragraphs and a conclusion. This is the basic *macro* structure followed by most response essays with maybe some variations depending on the requirement of the structure. Research essays have a different structure suitable to their requirement. We will discuss this structure later in the chapter. *Meso* refers to the organization of content at the paragraph level. This pertains to the fact that each paragraph must hold a logical position in the overall flow of the essay through its content and link to the information above as well as below it. It should essentially cohere with the rest of the essay. *Micro* level planning is applicable at the sentence and diction level. The choice of words and expression chosen to articulate should be relevant to the topic and appropriate to its style and tone.

In this chapter we are looking mainly at the *macro* and the *meso* organization of essays. *Micro* planning depends on the topic chosen, the subject of study, the purpose of presentation and the target audience. This makes for a separate study which requires a different focus. Let us start with discussing the macro and micro level structures in response essays first.

In a response essay the most basic and widely accepted structure of presentation is the introduction, body paragraph and conclusion format. Let us look at each of these elements one by one.

## Introduction

Whenever two or more people meet, introductions are customary. In keeping with the practice, an introduction to a piece of writing sets the stage for an effective and fruitful communication between the writer and the reader.

The purpose of the introduction is to help the reader start preparing a framework based on the preliminary information received so that s/he is able to connect with the text at a deeper level while progressing through the write up. Before a reader gets involved with the text, it is important to attract his or her attention to the same. The techniques that are employed to achieve this purpose are called a 'hook' which act to 'hook on' the reader to the text. These are:

- An **anecdote** which is a brief story which introduces the topic in an interesting way and also provides a base for the writer's claim later on in the paragraph. The story so narrated makes a point and from that point stems the author's argument.

  "Once as I sat in my house in a high-rise building of 22 flats, the building alarm bell indicating the start of a fire rang. I was on the $10^{th}$ floor. The lifts had stopped working as a safety measure and we were about a 1000 of us going down the stairs in a rush to be safe. It was a struggle pushing myself through the crowd while at the same time letting the aged and the children go past to safety first. By the time I reached the assembly point, the alarm had stopped. It was a fire safety drill and I had failed to reach the safe zone within the stipulated time. It is then that I thought. Are low rise buildings safer to live in than high rise ones? To reach a conclusion, let us compare and contrast low-rise and high-rise buildings on the criteria of safety in case of natural calamities, man created adversity and security from intruders and unwanted guests."

  It is good idea to first identify a stance on the topic and then think of a suitable anecdote to introduce it. However, here the stance is mentioned after the anecdote.

- **A Startling fact or statement** is another means to catch the reader's attention. Such a start shocks the reader into carrying on reading.

  "According to a study by Harvard professor, David Wise, and two colleagues, 46.1% of Americans die with less than $10,000 in assets. Will we still say that Americans are the richest people in the world? No, in my opinion Asians are the richest people in the world even though they live in poor countries. Let us analyze this claim in the light of the taxes collected, existence of liquid money in the economy and possession of gold."

- **A Famous quote or paraphrase** can also be used to attract a reader to engage with a text.

  "Mughal King, Jehangir, rightly stated that if there is heaven on earth anywhere, it is only in Kashmir. It is one of the most pristine and arresting places in the world with its outstretched green valleys ensconced between magnificent snow-covered peaks. It is a place one must visit at least once in a lifetime. This essay describes Kashmir in terms of its scenic bounty, warm milieu and approachability for travel."

- Asking a **rhetorical question** is another popular way of starting an introduction. A rhetorical question is one that is asked to create a dramatic effect or to make a point rather than to receive an answer.

  "How many of you have never lied to save yourself? Maybe no one. We all lie to save ourselves from difficult situations, to avoid trouble or simply just for fun. Why then do we still teach our children that one should never lie when actually we don't believe in what we say? I believe to lie is good and necessary at times. In this essay, I will give you three instances when lying or hiding the truth which is also a kind of lie, our scriptures say, is good."

These are some ways in which a reader can be lured to read a text. These techniques can be used individually or in combinations as per the choice and prowess of the writer.

Other than attracting a reader to a text, another matter which must be carefully handled is establishing a common understanding of the topic between the writer and the reader. A communication is smooth and fruitful only if the reader and the writer are at the same level of understanding with the topic being written about. Once that is established, the reader is able to fruitfully construct knowledge using the information laid out in the text and indulge in a gainful reading experience. To institute this common ground, the writer may either define, explain, or state relevant details in the introductory paragraph to an essay. Sometimes, writers even enunciate what the topic does not mean or connote to bring home the desired perception. Once a general understanding has been instituted, the writer can move on to the specific idea being addressed.

Further to creating a common understanding of possibly ambiguous terms and concepts related to the theme or the topic, the introductory section is also used to build the background knowledge of the reader. The writer must assess the basic information that the reader needs to have in order to understand and possibly agree with the writer and use the introduction to provide that enlightenment to the reader. To decide what background information to provide and how much of it to provide, requires careful thought and selection. More than the needed amount may confuse the reader and dilute the focus of the argument. For instance, if the writer is presenting his or her claim regarding Article 370 of the Indian constitution, a reader must know what the particular article says and what amendments, if any, have been proposed to the same to be able to relate to what the writer is presenting.

The introduction to an essay is incomplete without a thesis or theme statement. The thesis statement clearly outlines to the reader what areas of the topic will be covered by the essay. It sets the boundaries of the essay and gives it a direction. The thesis statement also gives the reader an opportunity to assess the essay and evaluate whether it has addressed the areas delineated in the theme statement or not. It also limits the exploration of the topic to a manageable threshold. To sum up, we can say that the introduction prepares the reader to receive the knowledge laid out in the following paragraphs successfully.

### Body Paragraphs

These are the most important sections of a piece of Academic writing. They develop the idea initiated in the introduction. To develop a paragraph means to delve deeper into the idea. It is in the body paragraphs that we find the content that the writer wants to convey. The claim on the topic along with the information and evidence related to the claim are all presented as a part of a paragraph. It is here that research findings are presented, discussed and analyzed. The Cambridge Academic

Content dictionary defines a paragraph as "a short part of a text, consisting of at least one sentence and beginning on a new line. It usually deals with a single event, description, idea etc." It is an important aspect of the organization of content.

Most paragraphs start with a topic sentence. This topic sentence is an important part of the paragraph as it links the paragraph itself to the thesis statement mentioned earlier as well as lays out the main idea of the paragraph which is also known as the controlling idea. The topic sentence holds much weight in a paragraph since it not only links the paragraph to the theme, but also substantiates the author's claim on the topic, provides a framework for the paragraph and gives thrust and focus to the development of content within the framework. It also gives the reader a sense of the content and stance of the paragraph since readers normally read the first few lines to gauge the bent of the write up and their interest in the same. In most instances the topic sentence is the first sentence of the paragraph. However, there are cases when this is not true. Sometimes, the first sentence is used to link the current paragraph to the previous one or to provide some background knowledge to enable the reader to comprehend the content in the current paragraph. In such cases, the topic sentence becomes either the second or the third statement. If a paragraph narrates a series of events or continues with information to support the topic sentence of the previous paragraph, there is no topic sentence in the paragraph. However, in most cases the presence of a topic sentence is seminal.

There are two parts to a topic sentence, the topic and the controlling idea which is the author's stance on or opinion about the topic. It is important that the topic sentence be clear and precise rather than general else its purpose of existence stands defeated. The following are some examples of the same:

1. Online education is good.
2. Online education has helped knowledge to reach students in every nook and corner of the world.

The subjects of both the topic statements is 'online education', but while the latter makes a specific remark on it which can be further developed in the paragraph, the former has a very general approach with no instruction on the course of expansion for the paragraph. It is for this reason that these kind of topic sentences should be avoided. The 'specific remark' in the sentence is what we call the 'controlling idea'. The controlling idea can be the writer's opinion or belief about the thematic content or may reflect the writer's attitude towards the topic. Once the reader acquaints himself/herself with the controlling idea, s/he is able to get a picture of what to expect in the paragraph and hence connects better with the content. On a lighter note, the controlling idea is the king in the paragraph and any sentence which does not provide information in relation to it either in the form of a supporting detail or evidence, is not allowed into the paragraph. Establishment of such an order is called coherence which will be discussed in greater detail in chapter six.

Once the topic sentence with the controlling idea has been written, the supporting details come into the picture. These are the details which are central to a paragraph being meaningful and of value. These supporting details can be expressed in multiple ways. These are:

1. *The explanation of a stance*. This means that the claim of the writer is explained in simpler terms along with throwing greater light on the assumptions made while taking the mentioned position. If the writer refers to some concept or information that may not be common knowledge, the writer must give an explanation of the same. In the same strain, if there is any concept or phenomenon which is not well-known, it may be interpreted differently. Hence, the writer must make it a point to explain his or her point of view and bring the reader to his or her thought level.
2. An anecdote, a story, a personal experience, etc. to illustrate the point being made in action. This narration must be linked to the claim being made and, in a way channelized through the story.
3. Some valid and relevant statistics as evidence in support of the stated finding. It is important to explain and interpret these evidences and link them to the claim being made.

4. Important contributions or noteworthy observations of experts or established researchers on the idea being supported either expressed as a quote or as a paraphrase.
5. A summary of another related and important survey or research conducted along with its findings and conclusion.
6. Definition of the concept along with an explanation where required, keeping in mind the audience being addressed through the writing and some examples of the same. The author can also choose to introduce the boundaries related to the application of the concept.
7. A synthesis of two or more discussions, interviews or talks related to the topic and the controlling idea made by known theorists and scholars to deduce a new thought or concept in support of the point made.
8. An example which drives home the point being made in the claim. This can be in the form of a short story or a fact.

There are several patterns that can be adopted to organize the supporting content in a paragraph depending on the topic and the objectives that the writer wants to achieve by writing the piece. Though there are no rules to control the choice of these patterns, sometimes suitability of a pattern to the content being presented plays a role while making a choice. The following are some of the patterns that may be identified for a better organization of the supporting content.

## A. Chronology

Chronology is said to be observed when the information presented is in the order of a progression in time, either backwards or forward. The objective of the author when using this pattern of organization is to take the reader through a journey in time. For example, a paragraph discussing the topic sentence, "Since 1936 when the first programmable computer was made, the computer industry has achieved many milestones."

A chronological order essentially calls for stating events in a time order, either forward or backwards. When using this pattern of organization, each section presents information related to a specific period of time. There are major supporting details which set out the time period being discussed followed by several minor secondary details related to the time period identified. Such a pattern of organization is followed in write ups which trace the development of a concept or an entity.

While adhering to the chronological pattern, the time order of events is important, and any change would either alter the meaning or cause confusion in comprehension. Some linking words which are commonly used are *after*, *afterwards*, *initially*, *at first*, *lastly*, *later into the day/night*, *on time*, *since*, *while*, *when*, *now*, *soon* etc.

### B. Sequentially

This pattern of organization is followed to present a sequence of events. It is similar to a chronological order in its approach though it calls for organization of content in a step by step process. This order of stating details in a paragraph is adopted when the author's purpose is to lay down or explain the process of an activity, stages to be followed to make an achievement or steps to be followed to reach a destination. While using this order of organization, use of transition expression like *first*, *next*, *at the end*, *to start with*, *followed by this*, etc. are often used.

### C. Spatially

More often than not, the spatial order is used to describe people, places, events or things. It has a starting point and moves in one direction forward or sideways as is preferred by the writer. This pattern is best suited when the author wants the reader to construct a mental picture of what is being described. It describes the elements of a subject in terms of their existence in relation to each other in placement. It is primarily used to write on topics which address the 'where' questions.

While using this pattern linking expressions like *next to, outside, near, around, close to, across, behind, adjacent, beyond, opposite, beside* etc. are used frequently.

**D. Order of Importance**

This pattern is used to talk about factors, aspects, causes, or theories associated with a concept. This pattern states that the most important elements being referred to should be mentioned and discussed first followed by the one which is next in importance. Essentially, it involves the mentioning of points in their declining order of importance. An opposite pattern also exists which is called the climactic order. This order entails stating the least important element first and the most important last so as to end with a lasting impression.

The pattern conforming to the order of importance is mostly followed while discussing the causes of a phenomenon or the effect of an action or happening. It can also be used while talking about advantages and disadvantages. The commonly used linking words are: *the most important*, *last but not the least*, *another*, *yet another*, *furthermore*, *additionally* etc.

Having discussed the content and the organization of the middle part of a paragraph, now let us now talk about the last statement of the same which we call the concluding statement. The chief role of this concluding statement is two-fold. One, the most important one, is to link the paragraph to the theme of the essay or to the following paragraph. Two, it is to indicate to the reader that the paragraph has ended. The concluding remark can be written in multiple ways. It can either restate the theme statement or summarize and reiterate the main focus of the paragraph. Additionally, it can draw a conclusion based on the information provided in the paragraph or state an observation in the context of the controlling idea. Furthermore, it can also make a prediction resting on the knowledge imparted earlier. If suitable to the discussion in the paragraph, the author can also express an opinion on the topic and the controlling idea as the final remark.

That the paragraph has ended must be indicated to the reader. This is done with the help of transition expressions like, *all in all*, *therefore*, *finally*, *in brief*, *in other words*, etc.

When constructing the body paragraphs, other than thinking about the claims on the topic related to the thesis statement, the supporting information to be provided along with valid evidences and the pattern of organization of the above, the writer must also mull over the transition expressions to be used which build in cohesion in the paragraph and hold its content together as a whole. The writer must also read the paragraph post writing to ascertain that the order decided upon has been effectively followed and the statements written give pertinent information on the topic and claim, add some intelligence to or state a contrasting view of the statements, give evidence in support, present statistics to corroborate the claim or relate an anecdote or a short story to reiterate the claim. Attention to the above stated aspects will ensure that the paragraph has been coherently written.

Other than the above, care must be taken that each paragraph has only one controlling idea on the topic. There should be a clear line of thought and all elements of the paragraph should efficiently link to that thought. It might also happen that though present in the mind, while writing the author has not included the controlling idea in the topic sentence. This must be attended to carefully as such a miss might lead to a directionless paragraph with an obscure line of presentation. Yet another essential element of paragraph writing is that whenever the writer provides statistics and data as supporting evidence, s/he must make it a point to explain how the data so stated connects with the controlling idea. A clarification and an inference must be included.

## Conclusion

What the concluding sentence does for the paragraph, the concluding paragraph does for the essay. It indicates to the reader that the essay has come to an end. It seeks to leave the reader with a final impact at the end of the reading. It picks up the loose threads in the essay and ties them together tightly. It works in a direction opposite to the introduction. Hence it starts with the specific approach discussed in the essay and ends with a general take stemming from the same.

It is a good idea to start the concluding paragraph with a rephrasing of the thesis statement. This beginning suggests to the reader that the writer has achieved what s/he had set out to achieve. However, simply restating the thesis statement would be of no avail. What would be useful is the adding of a new and deeper understanding while rephrasing the thesis statement. This new information should have its base in the discussion that has been previously laid out. Care should be taken that no new point or idea is introduced in the essay at this stage. The supporting sentences in the body of the concluding paragraph are normally reworded topic sentences of the body paragraphs which serve to highlight the dominant points of discussion. The closing sentence in the concluding paragraph must leave the reader with a sense of finality and closure on the topic of debate. The ultimate statement must leave the reader with a thought to mull over or demonstrate the importance of the writer's position on the topic. It must end on a positive note and leave the reader with a sense of learning and satisfaction at having read the essay.

An interesting way to ensure ending with a great concluding remark is to answer how the thought, position or claim being discussed impacts the reader or the target audience in general. This will give the reader a sense that s/he has read something important and learnt something that should be known. Other effective ways to end the concluding paragraph is to propose a course of action, suggest looking for a solution if applicable or raise a question for further study.

Understanding the purpose and structure of the introductory, body and concluding paragraphs goes a long way to help the writer to put together a potent yet interesting response essay. The paragraphs in the different kinds of response essays have their own suitable paragraph organization which will be discussed in the following chapter when we talk about the different response essays in detail.

## IMRaD

Defining a scientific or any other research article, O'Conner and Woodford said,

> A scientific or research article or paper is a technical... document that describes a significant experimental, theoretical or observational extension of current

> knowledge, or advances in the practical application of known principles. (p. 108)

As stated earlier, such research-based articles or essays have a different format and manner of presentation based on their purpose and communication requirement. T. Hengl and M. Gould also described research articles, henceforth referred to as RA, as follows,

> Unlike a novel, a newspaper article or an essay, an RA has a required structure and style, which is by international consensus known as "Introduction Methods Results and Discussion" or IMRaD. However, a RA is not only a technically rigid document, but also a subjective intellectual product that unavoidably reflects personal opinions and beliefs. Therefore, it requires good skills in both structuring and phrasing the discoveries and thoughts. These skills are acquired through experience, but can also be taught.

Writing compliant with the IMRaD model follows the 'wine glass approach' or the 'hourglass approach' to present its content, as given by Hilary Glasman-Deal.

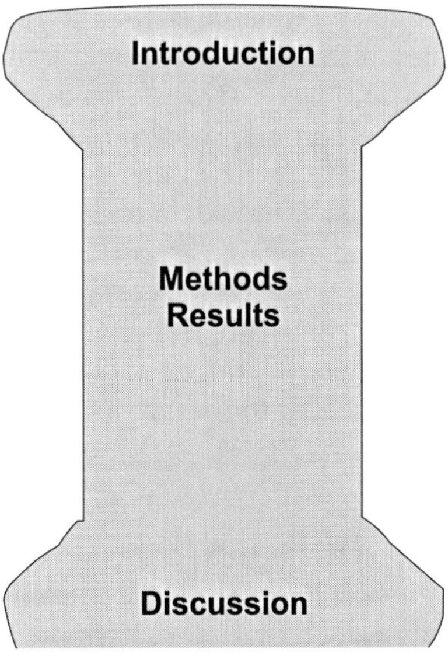


https://kib.ki.se/en/write-cite/academic-writing/structure-academic-texts

The model has two noteworthy characteristics which are indicative of the direction of the plot laid out in the article. One characteristic is the 'top-bottom symmetrical shape, and the other is the 'change in width'. The former characteristic is representative of the fact that an RA starts with a general talk on the topic and gradually comes to the specific research hypothesis being studied. The focus moves from a broad angle to a narrow approach. The paper consistently maintains that approach while discussing the methods used for research and the results obtained. It finally extrapolates the findings in the specific area of research in a larger context. It is important to note here that like in a response essay, the introduction and the conclusion are reverse in their attitude to the topic. The change in width noticed in the diagram shows the change in the perspective from general to specific and back. The model fundamentally follows the flow that a scientific study follows. Let us look at each section of IMRaD in greater detail.

While planning for writing a research article, it would be gainful to consider Richard Fulkerson's STAR model which is an acronym for Sufficient, Typical, Accurate and Relevant. 'Sufficient' simply means that the materials referred to should be ample so as to make available enough information to write. The researcher should consult an adequate number of researches to glean common findings; 'Typical', communicates that the material read and consulted should offer information that people from the field can relate to and comprehend with ease; 'Accurate', conveys that it is understood that every researcher looks for accurate and updated statistics. Finally, 'Relevant', alludes to the fact that scholarly sources pertaining to the topic of research should be consulted and referred to for supporting the claim. The time period to which such referenced work belongs should also not be too far away from the time of the proposed research.

## Introduction

Similar to the introductory paragraph in the response essays, the introduction here orientates the reader to effectively contextualize and receive the knowledge laid out ahead in the

RA. It is essential that the writer start with introducing the topic in perspective so that the reader can create a related schema and be gradually made to focus on the upcoming research details to understand and relate to its importance and impact in the concerned field of study. To facilitate the creation of such a schema it is a good idea to introduce the topic with the help of a common context, something which the reader is likely to have known or observed. The importance of research on this topic in the present times must also be established. One way to do this is to add quotes which support the relevance and significance of the author's case. These quotes can be supplemented with a paraphrase of another author's statement to hold up the writer's claim regarding the importance of the topic or a comment on the critical need of the finding of a solution to the gap identified. The writer can also synthesize the results obtained by two or more researches to come to a conclusion and identify an opportunity for a further study which is being engaged in through the current paper.

With the substance of what is being done fully established, it is time to bring the reader on board with the information needed to connect with the research. For this relevant background information about the topic along with related research initiatives undertaken by well-known academicians and researchers must be outlined in the introductory part of the paper. The reader should be provided with all the information that she or he needs to understand the claim and explanation of the writer and get a complete picture of what has been done in the field so far, as well as know to what extent the gaps have been identified. The research must be purported as one that fills the gap so identified, either partly or wholly. The way the presence of a gap is highlighted is also important. Look at the following example:

> Although the effect of rubber particles on the mechanical properties of co-polymer systems has been demonstrated over two years ago, little attention has been paid to the selection of an appropriate rubber component. (Glasman-Deal, p. 22)

This statement clearly identifies the gap in the research on the topic so far. The reader has been apprised of the related research and is able to place the importance and purpose of the current research in context.

Care should be taken to select and choose the researchers whose works are quoted in the introduction. The purpose of stating the previously done research work is to help the reader to draw up a research map in his or her mind regarding who the key players in the field are and what progress or achievement has been made so far. Areas of the field which have been researched in, areas which have unanswered questions despite rigorous research and domains which have unexplored sections must also be brought to the notice of the leader. This allows the reader to place the current research initiative in the mental map created for the progress and discern its relationship with the cited works in the field.

There are two facets to be considered when collecting information on the background of the research topic. One is the reason why this should be done and the other is the ways in which it could be done. There are three reasons why background information needs to be given along with relevant research studies that have been undertaken in the area along with successes and failures. One, the reader must have all the knowledge needed to connect with the topic and relate to the author's concern. Two, the reader must understand the importance of the research and the purpose of study in the chosen area. The research receives the reader's support only when the latter comprehends its need as well as its criticality in the current scenario. This perception has to be built in the mind of the reader by means of referring to the various studies that have been conducted and how they have failed to find the answers which this research initiative seeks to identify. Finally, it must be communicated to the reader that the writer has read all or most of the literature available on the topic of research and has taken reasoned steps towards isolating the topic of study. It also assures the reader that the research topic is novel and is not repeating some or most parts of a study done earlier.

Let us now explore the ways in which various research endeavours can be mentioned in the introduction. Those researches which are well-known, and the results of which have been discussed and accepted and have high credibility can be quoted with a clear research reference. However, some findings or data which have been discussed generally with no clear research background can also be mentioned as literature on the topic as areas which are being looked into along with names of researchers who are planning to so indulge. Having said this, the writer also needs to decide how to organize the literature in the section. One way to do so is chronological. The writer can choose to start with the most relevant and milestone research in the past and move forward to describe the current scene. Another way to lay out the literature is to group the different methodologies, approaches or models used based on a criterion, e.g., time period, and mention them in chunks. It is the writer's discretion to adopt one of these ways to discuss the developments in a field based on his or her comfort, requirement of the topic or simply choice.

Next comes the statement of purpose in the paper. Having discussed the topic of interest in general, it is imperative that the writer states the specific area of research being proposed as the direct solution to the concern or one of the possible solutions to the same. It is crucial that the author set the focus of the paper very clearly. Once the problem has been spelt out the writer must state what his or her point of view is regarding what a solution can be through a hypothesis. It is the viability and impact of this hypotheses which will be researched and discussed further in the RA. Once the hypothesis is stated, a brief description of what the researcher plans to do to work with the hypothesis that is given.

Glasman-Deal proposes a model with four components to be followed when writing a research paper.

---

1 Establish the importance of your field
  Provide background facts/information (possibly from research)
  Define the terminology in the title/keywords
  Present the problem area/current research focus

2 Previous and/or current research or contributions

3 Locate a gap in the research
Describe the problem you will address
Present a prediction to be tested

4 Describe the present paper

---

Another model, popularly known as the CARS model (Creating A Research Space) was developed by John Swales in 1990 which can be followed to write an effective introduction to a RA. This model was developed post detailed studies of various journal articles in a variety of disciplines. The model, like the Glasman-Deal model seeks to explain and describe the organization of content in the introductory section of the research paper. Swales believed that writing the introduction to a research paper is the most difficult part of the authoring. His model hopes to successfully guide the authors to produce robust introductions.

In the CARS model, Swales talks of three moves which almost all researchers make. Move one is 'establishing a territory'. It proposes that the author must establish that the area of research chosen is relevant in the current times and is important as well as interesting. To do so the author must follow three steps. The first step is to 'claim centrality'. This means that that the topic of research must be highlighted as an area of recent activity in terms of study and one which is significant enough to be researched. Step two is to make topic generalizations. This requires the writer to provide background knowledge on the topic. The writer could take the reader on the path of development that the topic has seen through the years and make him or her aware of the milestones attained. This leads us to step three which requires the writer to discuss the related and relevant previous studies in a way that the reader is acquainted with the credible and critical achievements made. While citing the research of others, the writer can choose to include the names of the researchers within the text (*integral citation*) or mention the names at the end in brackets. (*nonintegral citation*).

In the second move, the author highlights the gaps that have been left in the research done so far and bares an open 'niche' in the topic that needs to be probed into. This move establishes the need for further investigation on the topic. The author can establish a 'niche' in any one of the following the three ways. One is to refute or challenge the claim of an earlier research through a counter claim. Another way is to foreground a gap in the existing knowledge and propose a study to bridge the same. Yet another way to identify a niche is to raise a question on the pronouncements of an established finding and propose additional research. A fourth way to ratify the niche is to accept a current study report but state the need for more information on the topic and call for continued research. A fifth way to create a niche is to seek to apply someone else's findings to a new area of the same topic or a new topic altogether.

Finally, the writer makes the third move. This move entails the writer's conversion of the established niche into the research space that she or he will fill up. The writer can do this in multiple ways. She or he can either state the purpose of the current study or straight away go onto discussing how the proposed research will contribute to the deliberations on the topic in the future. The author is expected to give a brief of the upcoming research so as to give a bird's eye view of the thesis to the reader. Basically, through this move the writer is making an effort to convince the reader of the importance of the current research work.

Both the models considered above are valid and acceptable models of leading a writer to structure the introduction of a research paper. Either can be chosen based on the comfort, familiarity, and preference of the researcher. Since this section of the thesis serves to persuade and engage the reader with the concerned work, the use of active voice is preferred.

## Materials and Methods

The introduction having been discussed in detail, let us now move onto the second section of the IMRaD model, which is, methodology. The purpose of this section is to inform the reader that the methods being followed, and the material being used are based on an agreed protocol. It examines the process followed to conduct the research. It essentially answers what, why and how of every step that is followed to orchestrate the research. The scholar is expected to mention the quality and quantity of the sample along with the reasons for choosing the sample and its size. The controlled, dependent, and independent variables must also be mentioned so that the impact can be measured as accurately as possible. The process followed must be mentioned to the most miniscule detail too. The measure of a good 'methodology' section is that it should be so well traced that the reader is able to follow it to get the stated result every time with possible minute but inconsequential variations, depending on the area of study. Essentially, it should show the reader the distinct path followed to arrive at the result. Owing to this expectation, the instructions and the steps mentioned in the paper must be clear and specific. If the method requires a sequence to be followed, care should be taken to use appropriate linkers along with a suitable formatting pattern to indicate the order of events or activities to be performed to avoid any confusion. Any assumptions made for the study must also be stated with precision to allow the reader's views to be synchronised with the author's line of thought.

Before explaining how the process of research was carried out, it would be a wise choice to discuss the method being followed for the research. Some general information about the technique being followed along with some knowledge on why it was chosen, familiarizes the reader with the course of activities elucidated ahead in the section and helps him or her engage with the paper better. Once the study methods have been discussed, it is important to talk about the study materials. Facts on which materials were chosen and why are integral to this part of the paper. Specific and detailed information on the attributes or components, as the case may be, of the materials that led to them being chosen for the research is very important too. This data allows for the reader to use alternatives in case the original material used in the stated experiment is not available. Further details include how the properties of the material and the different elements of research are manipulated to reach the desired results, whether they actually yield results or not is another matter. Another major intelligence that must be mentioned here is the procedure followed to measure the findings and the format of the presentation. Such knowledge allows for an efficacious replication of the research. Yet another important inclusion in this section is a statement of the problems that were faced through the course of the experiment. The author must mention whether the problems could be solved or not. If the problems were resolved, how was it done as well as how did it impact the findings? In case the issue could not be resolved, how did it impact the outcome of the experiment?

One organizational rule that must religiously be followed in a research paper is the use of sub-headings to allow for an enhanced comprehension of the stages and the flow. Here the writer is likely to use the past tense in the passive form since a series of past actions are being reported in an objective manner.

### Results

As is evident from the title, the objective of this section is to lay down the detailed results of the research carried out in a logical order. This is the most important section of the paper which gives the researching scholars an opportunity to showcase his or her contribution to the concerned field of study.

There might be a series of results that surface at the end of an experiment. It is the author's discretion to decide the order of the presentation of the results. The author might also decide to foreground some findings while relegate some others to the background. The highlighted outcome might be one that is more important to the field and one that introduces a novel learning in the area which enriches the quality of discussions and debates on the topic. Certain minor or inconsequential findings in the context of the hypothesis being considered should not be released so that the focus on the primary results is not diluted in anyway.

Another aspect that is considered while releasing the results obtained from an experiment is how conclusive they are. If the result supports a definitive conclusion in relation to the hypothesis, it is an important finding.

It is advised that the writers use varied drawings, diagrams, charts, figures, or tables to organize and present the data in a manner that supports the writer's story. It is important to carefully categorize the information in a way that makes the findings lucidly available for the reader to notice and grasp. For this, it is imperative to present the data in the same order as the methods in the section above whose results are being outlined here. A statistical analysis indicating the finding can also be included. It is also critical to include an interpretation of the symbols or signs used, if any. Apart from this any aberrations or variance observed in the responses of the sample group(s) should be reported along with an information on how it has impacted the figures. In case of multiple findings that need to be reported, much discretion should be practised in the presentation of all the results with a well-structured explanation for each category. That the results are perceived with clarity and as supporting the hypothesis is important for the success of the research initiative.

## Discussion

This is another significant section of a research paper where the above stated results are interpreted and, as the name suggests, discussed. Essentially, it explains to the reader what the results arrived at mean. The writer uses this section to summarize the main findings of the research and connect them to the study previously done. The writer explains how the results either bridge the gap identified and accentuated in the introduction, or extend a set of studies carried out in the past, or present a new perspective to an earlier discovery or introduce a completely new aspect of the researched area. The author also explains any anomaly or any variation from the expected results that might have been observed while collating the results of the experiment. A data can have multiple interpretations. The author must extend his or her thought to recognize what these could be and mention them here along with any qualifying remark that needs to be made to place the interpretation in perspective. The author must also state why the interpretation she or he has deduced is the most valid and acceptable. In case the research is based on a question raised on the findings of another study on a similar topic, it becomes imperative for the researcher writing the paper to institute a comparison between the current research and the previously held ones, especially the one that has been questioned to state in what way the current study has added or improved upon the earlier statistics.

Though the major findings of the study are the focal point of the result declaration, some minor findings may be meaningful and might need to be explained after being mentioned categorically in the results section. The meaning these findings convey and the implications they might have in the area of research must be well-expounded. It goes without saying that the impact of the main discoveries must be clearly elucidated too along with application limitations, if any. Both weak as well as the strong aspects of the research must be discussed in detail along with any caveats that might be important to note.

A critical role of this section is to extend the findings in this specific context to the broader context of the field. It is of prime significance to discuss how the findings of the current research illuminate aspects of the field which may have been completely ignored or may have been given less attention earlier. The author must also talk about how the data uncovered through this research impacts the overall understanding of the area and topic of the study. The practical implications of the research must also be explicated. It would make the author sound more credible if he or she took an initiative to state that the results obtained were not as conclusive as expected and raised the need for further research. The author may garner further acknowledgement if after identifying the presence of some unanswered questions post the completion of the research and an analysis of its results she or he proposes an extended research.

In the diagram representing the IMRaD model we see that the discussion block is an exact reversal of the introduction chunk. While the latter follows a general to specific approach, the former moves from specific to general. It picks up the threads of the specific study conducted and uses them to lend a new understanding of the field in general.

This leads us to the conclusion of the essay wherein the author clearly states if the findings proved the hypothesis strengthened, weakened, completely justified or falsified. In each case a future course of action as well as the current implications on the topic must be detailed. Care should be taken not to introduce any new aspect of either the research or the result in this part of the essay. The essay ends with a succinct yet all-inclusive summary of the research article.

The IMRaD is a widely adopted and accepted model for research articles. According to Meadows (1985, 1998), changing the internal organization of research papers is one way for the scientific community to respond to the expeditious growth of scientific information. The IMRaD is a result of this evolution. With the passage of time the content in the various fields of study has grown exponentially. A lot of research has been conducted to create new knowledge and understanding. The IMRaD was developed to allow the future researchers to incorporate all relevant data in future studies. The structure of the essay follows the logic of the research process and seeks to support the scholar in presenting his or her work in a well-structured manner. However, there have been variations that have been introduced in the structure. Some researchers find it more convenient to club the results and the discussion section. They feel it is better to state results along with an explanation of their meaning, strengths, weaknesses, and impact rather than revisit them in a different section of the essay. While here we have talked about the concluding paragraph as a separate entity, some writers include it in the discussion segment and treat the discussion as the logical end to the article. Some other researchers may want to call the 'discussion' segment as 'analysis' and the 'discussion' may actually be the conclusion. Yet another variation to the format has been observed in the form of a separate section on literature review after the introduction, not as a part of the same.

Some of the established merits of the IMRaD framework are that it offers a well-defined structure for researchers to present their work. It makes a provision for all the relevant information that must be included for a complete and meaningful reception of the study. It does not allow for unnecessary and distracting data or content to be included and helps the writer streamline the presentation of his or her research results. Since the form is well-recognized as a format for the display of research findings, it creates an immediate understanding in the mind of the readership and awards credibility to the work. It is the result of a long process of evolution from the 17th century onwards when the first research paper was written. Its design allows the writer to demonstrate his or her knowledge of the related and relevant literature, lay out the process of research as well as share the results obtained along with giving an opportunity to discuss perspectives and deductions as perceived by the researcher. Even though it has a tight system in place, it permits variations to factor in an author's choices or preferences. Essentially, it allows the writer to express his or her point of view in detail and make an impact in the area of research. Discussing the journey of its dominance in research presentation, Carmen Pérez-Llantada says that IMRaD which was originally devised for the presentation of biomedical research has rapidly spread to other areas of study. She further adds that this format started to be used as the chosen organizational structure for the biomedical and health sciences in 1940 and by 1980s became the only valid way to present an original research work. Though the authors who adopted this format were unable to give a reason for adopting this design yet they acknowledged that it facilitates modular reading which is the kind of reading most of the readership indulges in, which is to look for information they need in sections of the paper. Mainly, it allows for scanning or looking for specific information which supports reader activity in a paper.

Though the IMRaD structure has many benefits, it has some caveats too. Some research scholars believe that the IMRaD format is too simplistic to be burdened with the responsibility of carrying the information of an entire research process. Moreover, to function within set boundaries can curtail and limit the discretion and creativity of a writer in showcasing his or her initiative and its results to the people. Peter Medawar criticized the structure for not providing a realistic representation of the thought process of a researcher. Another limitation often cited against the IMRaD format is that it may not be suitable for the presentation of qualitative researches.

In this chapter both the response essays as well as the research essays, also called research articles, have been discussed in detail. A close examination of the two organizational patterns reveals that they are quite similar in their setting though the terminology used may be different. For example, the method and results sections of the research essay are akin to the body paragraphs of a response essay. Though the content of the introduction and the conclusion passages may be different, the purpose of these sections in both the kinds of essays is the same. Before the students are assigned a task to write either kind of an essay, it is imperative to discuss the appropriate transition words and expressions, content words that must be used to indicate familiarity with the context and content as well as objective articulation. Knowledge of the language to be used as well as the inclusions to be made in the various sections as delineated in this chapter will aid the students to produce academically sound essays.

## Works Cited

Glasman-Deal, Hilary. *Science Research Writing for Non-Native Speakers of English*. World Scientific, 2010, *books.google.co.in*, books.google.co.in/books?id=sehpDQAAQBAJ&printsec=frontcover&dq=inauthor:"Hilary+Glasman-Deal"&hl=en&sa=X&ved=0ahUKEwjVoMC4n57lAhWHvI8KHXtCBIkQ6AEIKDAA#v=onepage&q&f=false.

Hengl, Tomislav, and Michael Gould. "Rules of Thumb for Writing Research Articles." *Researchgate.net*, 2002, www.researchgate.net/publication/228549945_RULES_OF_THUMB_FOR_WRITING_RESEARCH_ARTICLES.

Saldanha, Gabriela, and Sharon O'Brien. *Research Methodologies in Translation Studies*. Routledge, 2015.

Singh, Anneliese A., and Lauren Lukkarila. *Successful Academic Writing: A Complete Guide for Social and Behavioral Scientists*. The Guilford Press, 2017.

Swales, John. *Genre Analysis: English in Academic and Research Settings*. Cambridge University Press, 2011.

Sahni, Peush, and Rakesh Aggarwal, editors. *Reporting and Publishing Research in the Biomedical Sciences*. Springer, Singapore, 2018.

# 5
# Types of Academic Texts

Every kind of writing has a purpose and so does Academic writing. This purpose can be either to present a new discovery identified, to describe a process, to put forth an understanding, to question an academic claim or to critically analyze a creative piece, a research finding or an academic claim. These purposes give birth to 'types' in Academic writing. This means that depending on what the purpose of a piece of writing is, we can categorize it into a type. Each type of Academic writing has content that must be presented in a suitable manner so that it achieves its purpose of communication with the intended audience. To acquire a complete comprehension of Academic writing it is imperative for an academician to know and understand in detail what these types are, as well as to discuss how the ideas, points or explanations presented in an essay or a report are organized.

We have talked about response and research writings in the previous chapter. In the present chapter, we will discuss the varied types of the two above-mentioned particular kinds of writing. Primarily there are the following kinds of response writing pieces that students at the school level are expected to produce: informative essays, descriptive essays, compare and contrast essays, argumentative essays, analytical essays, and evaluative essays. Laboratory Reports are also a kind of investigative writing that is generally a part of the science subjects in the middle school. Though students are also expected to write narrative essays as a part of their literary studies, yet we will not discuss them here as they belong to the genre of creative writing which is not within the purview of this book.

At a higher level, research takes place in both social sciences as well as the technical sciences and the presentation follows a somewhat different structure. Let us consider the various facets of each of these writing types exhaustively. There are some other essays that are less complicated in content and structure which will be discussed in brief. The previous chapter has propounded general information on how the content in an essay must be structured. In this chapter, we will re-visit the organization of subject matter in the context of the essay types considered.

## Response Essays

### 1. *Informative Essays*

The chief goal of an informative essay or an expository essay is to provide an in-depth knowledge of a person, object, belief, practice, event or phenomenon to its reader and educate him or her on the same. This knowledge can be in the form of a definition, description, comparison, elucidation, etc. Typically, an informative essay answers one or more of 'who', 'where', 'when', 'what', 'why', and 'how' about the topic. These kinds of essays are commonly associated with subjects like History, Geography, Science, Economics, etc.

The task that requires an informative essay in response can be set in two ways. One, a narrow topic is given. For example, causes of World War II. With this topic the writer does not need to choose a line of thought. It is a very straightforward topic which expects the learner to talk about the events or situations that led to the second World War. Two, a generic and broad topic is stated. For example, illegal immigration. In this case, the author is expected to identify a particular line of thought and provide relevant information on it in a logical manner. In this essay, the writer can choose to talk about the situation of illegal immigration in a particular nation or how process of illegal immigration is actuated. The essay can optionally give details about the causes of the activity in question or the consequences thereof.

Like other essays, an informative essay too begins with an introduction which encases the theme statement. Taking a cue from the theme statement, the body paragraphs present a discussion on the area of the topic identified. They state a fact or piece of information related to the topic and mentioned in the theme statement as the main idea and corroborate it with supporting details related to the fact to extend the information being disseminated through the essay. To further supplement the information, the writer can provide examples or give authenticated statistics. In informative essays it is important that the author has extensively read and researched the topic of writing to showcase a good understanding and knowledge level. A significant requirement of an informative essay is that the author must practice caution and resist from expressing his or her opinion on any aspect of the topic being considered in the essay. This is a platform for educating the reader not influencing him or her in anyway hence the writer must desist from weaving in his or her emotions or feelings related to the information being present into the essay. Though an indirect impact on the mind of the reader after reading the essay might be made, any direct effort towards achieving such an influence is to be discouraged. For a student to be able to practice such restraint, it is important that s/he be aware of the language that is used to express an opinion and that which is used to state a fact. Most times, a writer unintentionally conveys a fact in a way that it appears to be an opinion. Hence it is essential that students be trained and given practice in identifying a fact as different from an opinion. They must also be made to notice the distinctive use of language while expressing either of them individually.

Other than being able to distinguish between a fact and an opinion, there are some more elements that writers must be made aware of to prepare them to produce high quality informative essays. Authors must be especially aware of the transition expressions required to add information, present a contrast, to exemplify and to emphasize in particular, while the knowledge and understanding of the other linking phrases might be helpful.

To prepare for writing an informative essay it is a good idea to make a mind map before you start writing and fill in the information to be mentioned in the essay in points. The below given mind map is just a sample. It is not complete.

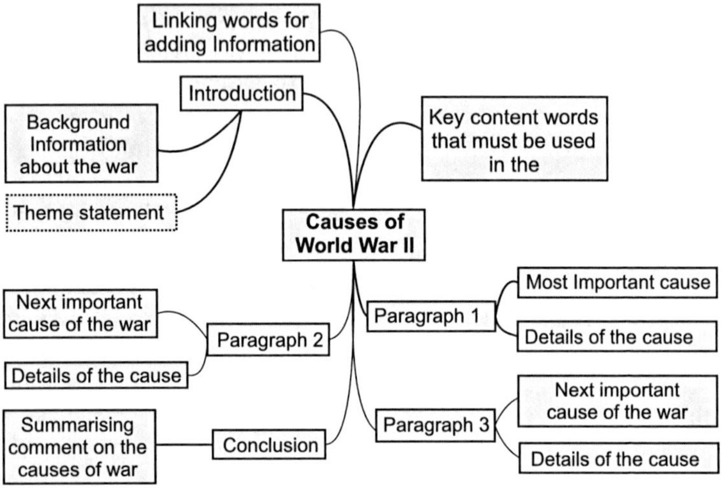


### 2. *Descriptive Essays*

A descriptive essay is a kind of informative essay which informs the reader on how a person, place, event or thing appears, smells, makes one feel, etc. depending on what is applicable. While describing, the author seeks to create a vivid and clear picture of the subject of description in the mind of the reader by appealing to the five senses of sight, sound, smell, touch, and taste. The primary tenet of a descriptive essay is 'Show, don't tell'. To follow this principle, the author uses figurative language like metaphors, simile, personification, alliteration, and other relevant devices to allow the reader to 'see' what the author is saying rather than just read. It is also essential for the writer to be aware of and use the appropriate and specific adjectives to describe the subject. Use of such adjectives allow for the creation of clear and discrete images as intended by the writer. However, before starting to write, an author should decide what kind of image s/he wants the reader to create about the subject. Depending on how the writer wants the reader to see the subject and what impression he or she wants to create in the mind of the reader about the subject, the author must brainstorm and choose the adjectives that are suitable for use.

There are two kinds of descriptive essays, objective and subjective. Objective essays are typically used in the technical and scientific subjects. They offer clear and factual descriptions of the subject without conveying the author's emotions. There is no use of figurative language or appeal to the senses. It is a factual description. On the other hand, we have the subjective essays which are mostly used with regard to the arts. The descriptions carry the author's perspective and emotions alongside the factual details and work towards making the reader see what the author has seen or wants him to see. The descriptions in this case have more to do with what the author sees them as rather than with what they actually might be. While writing a subjective account about a person, a place or an event a writer can choose to mix the two approaches, yet, one approach always dominates.

The layout of content in a descriptive essay can be done in multiple ways. It can either be a spatial arrangement, in order of importance, chronological or general to specific. An order or mode is chosen based on what the purpose of the writing is. In an essay describing a person, the writer can talk about the person's appearance, his or her achievements, character, and lifestyle and so many other things depending on who the target audience is. If the appearance is being discussed or the lifestyle and character, it is likely that the writer chooses the general to specific organization for the content. However, if the focus of the essay is a person's achievements, then the author might organize the content using the order of importance structure. In a descriptive essay that intends to describe a place, the essayist must first decide how he wants the place to be perceived. After a line of image is chosen, the author can either choose to adopt the general to specific approach to the description by first talking about the place on a broad level and then choosing specific areas to provide further details on or can choose the order of importance approach by talking about the most important aspects of the place along with stating specific facts about those aspects and moving further to not so important facets of the place. While writing descriptive details about a place, it is a good idea to start from one point and move in a logical manner in a particular direction.

An essay describing an object normally follows a general to specific pattern of presentation of content. The essay generally starts with talking about the general impression a reader might get on the first view of the object and then moves on to discussing its features, uses, functionality, etc. Describing an object commonly involves an objective outlook, however, if the objective is being described as being of special significance, then the writing can be expected to be subjective in its viewpoint as well as in articulation.

A descriptive essay is meant to either introduce a person, an object or a place to the reader either factually or through the writer's lens. While writing the latter kind, writers face the risk of using figurative language to a level where it become incomprehensible or too complicated to fulfil its chief purpose of educating the reader about the subject as an entity. Hence, the author must be careful to use a healthy mix of figurative and literal expression.

To be able to produce an effective descriptive essay, it is important that students be made aware of and be given adequate practice in the elements of useful figurative language. For example, they should know what personification is, how to use it, where to use it and what impact it can have on the audience. The same is needed for the other devices that make for figurative language. Learners should also have a wide and varied knowledge of adjectives and their degrees, adverbs, complements and adverbials. Awareness on the above-mentioned fronts will allow and equip a writer to construct a worthy descriptive essay.

### 3. *Compare and Contrast Essays*

Compare and contrast essays are a common form of Academic writing. While comparing two or more people, objects, places, events, ideas, theories, methods, processes, results, etc. we look at the similarities between them, whereas, while contrasting, we look at the differences. To be able to compare and contrast is a life skill which is developed and honed during school and college life to be used in the later years in authentic situations. There can be two purposes of writing a compare and contrast essay. One is to simply educate the reader about the similitude and divergence between two subjects and aid the reader in making an informed choice. The other reason is to develop critical thinking and analytical faculties.

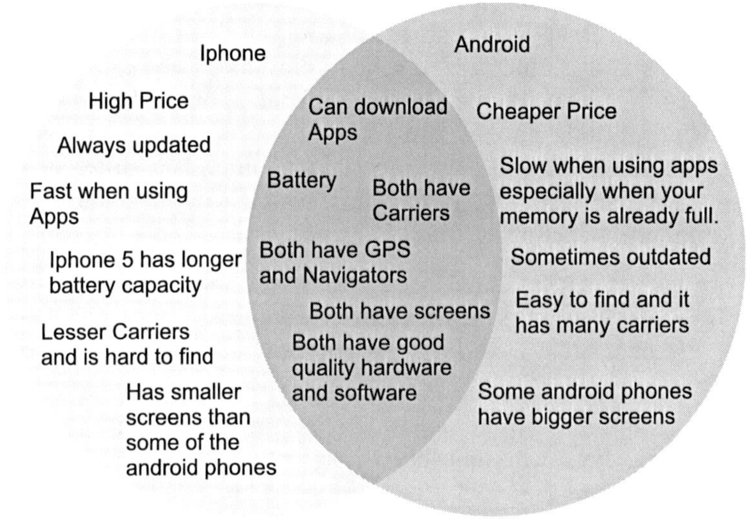


chrisheeroo.weebly.com

The most interesting compare and contrast essays are those that seek to present the likeness and distinction between two or more reasonably dissimilar subjects. However, subjects are comparable only if they have at least one common strain. For example, a common theme, a common perspective or a common medium of expression and the like. In keeping with the tradition of essay writing, a compare and contrast essay too begins with an introduction. An ideal introduction would make an effort to connect with the reader by providing some basic information about the two or more subjects being compared and highlighting the common thread between them. This also serves to bring the reader on the same thought lane as the writer and enables the reader to engage with the reading better. Ensconced within the introduction is the theme statement which clearly outlines the areas, criteria or aspects on which the comparison will be based. The theme statement gives the reader a frame within which the picture is created as the essay progresses. It is imperative that the author visit the thematic pronouncement repetitively so as to keep within the set frame.

Having written the introduction, the writer moves towards creating the body paragraphs. A good thing to do before starting to write the essay is to brainstorm and pen down the perceived sameness and distinctness in a Venn diagram. For example, we may compare an iPhone and an android phone. Though they both are mobile phones and have almost similar functions, a closer look of the issue may reveal some interesting differences. Look at the Venn diagram below which can be made as a planning tool before writing the actual essay.

Once the ideas have been put in writing, the author no longer needs to think of them and is rendered free to focus on the use of language, and the presentation and the organization of content.

The content in an essay discussing the similitude and divergence between subjects can be organized in three varied ways. They are the block, the point by point and the compare/contrast paragraphs methods. The block method calls for scrutinizing the elements of comparison and contrast as stated in the theme statement for each subject in a separate paragraph one after the other. No information about any other subject except the one being discussed should be mentioned in the respective paragraph. The positive quality of this method is that the writer is able to focus with complete attention on one subject at a time and may put forth a rich account of the subject while keeping within the frame set by the theme statement. However, the reader will be required to keep going back and forth between the paragraphs to get a clear grasp of the similarities and differences. In this form of organization, the role of the transition expressions becomes very important in the paragraphs discussing the second and the third subjects as they have to keep linking back to the related points in the previous body paragraph(s) to note the similarity or difference as the case may be. In fact, each paragraph following the first one should start with an appropriate linking word to indicate that in this paragraph a comparison with the previous one(s) is being presented. Another point to keep in mind is that the order of discussing the criterion mentioned in the theme statement should be the same in all the body paragraphs for the convenience of the reader.

Another approach to organizing a compare and contrast essay is the point wise structure. In this kind of an organization, each point of similitude or variance is treated as a separate entity and discussed in one paragraph. Typically, there are as many paragraphs as there are criteria since the comparison of the two or more subjects is based on the criteria. A chief presupposition of this organization pattern is that the writer has an adequate amount of content regarding each point, enough to write a reasonable sized paragraph. This method of laying out content makes for an easy read for the reader. There is little back and forth movement and all aspects to consider for a given criterion concerning all the subjects are at one place.

Yet another way of organizing content is to consider all the resemblance between the subjects in one paragraph and all the divergence in another. Accompanying points of similarity and contrariety are related and appropriate explanations and examples which help make complete meaning of the presentation. This pattern is normally followed when there is not much to write for each area. If we have a lot to write and we choose this format the paragraphs might become unwieldy and confusing beyond a point.

There is no hard and fast rule regarding the choice of an organization pattern. It is completely a matter of choice, comfort, and the writer's preference. However, it is important to remember to use linking expressions between paragraphs to make the text reader friendly. It is also essential that the similarities and differences discussed are subtle and unexpected to some extent and not just a stating of the more or less obvious disparities and likenesses.

The concluding paragraph in an essay ties the loose strings if any and revisits the entire discussion in brief. The writer might choose to add an opinion while writing the conclusion along with a paraphrased version of the theme statement. Yet, an opinion makes sense only if the purpose is to help the reader make an informed choice. In case the purpose is to enrich the readers' critical skills, it would make more sense to conclude the essay with a summary of the critical points discussed.

### 4. *Argumentative Essays*

An argumentative essay is yet another type of academic text widely encouraged to be written in schools and colleges with a view to developing the skill of making an informed opinion and presenting it supported by relevant and valid evidences and arguments. This kind of writing encourages the writer not only to think through his or her own reasoning and thoughts but also to consider those of the opponents. It further expects the writer to put forth ideas countering the opposition's anticipated viewpoints appropriately and convincingly and persuading the reader to accept and stand by the views of the writer. Before moving on to the paper with a pen, this kind of writing calls for careful investigation on a topic, framing a hypothesis, collecting of evidence in support of the hypothesis and testing it for authenticity and validity. It also involves making deductions regarding the hypothesis based on the evidence collected and finally arriving at a position on the topic. Such writing further involves inducing the reader to believe and agree with the writer on the position taken by the latter on the topic after reading the arguments framed and presented effectively.

Typically, an argumentative essay argues the validity of a fact in a given scenario, puts forth a new or different interpretation of an old-time belief or knowledge, establishes the importance of an action, thought, process, or method, elucidates the causes of a phenomenon or discusses the impact thereof. It might even propose solutions to an existing or a perceived problem.

Akin to the other academic essays, an argumentative essay too has an introductory paragraph which includes the thesis statement. Since in this genre of writing, the essay includes the opposing point of view along with the authors view, the thesis statement has the choice to reflect either just the author's position or both, that is, the author's stance as well as the opposing perspective. For example,

> "The most important quality needed to be successful is a positive attitude."
>
> "Though many people believe that focus and hard work ensure success in life, studies have proved that the most important quality needed to be successful, is a positive attitude."

Both the statements above are valid and acceptable thesis statements for an argumentative essay. They clearly spell out to the reader what will be discussed ahead.

The kind of essay being discussed here can be put together in three different ways. One is the normal classical manner which entails writing an introduction, body paragraphs, whose number depends on the number of supporting details that the writer has given if the organizational structure happens to be point by point, though a minimum of three body paragraphs is recommended and then a conclusion. While the introduction serves to introduce the essay with an appropriate hook, set out the boundaries for the discussion and if required, create a common understanding between the writer and the reader on the topic by stating the interpretation and assumptions of the writer or defining any ambiguous terms or concepts associated with the position being taken, the conclusion summarizes the entire discourse and at the same time emphasizes the main points to be noted in favour of the position that might help the reader to agree with the author. The conclusion, depending on the topic might also call for an action or attention, or may issue a warning to the reader as the closing remark.

Another model for an argumentative essay is Stephen Toulmin's model, called the Toulmin model. Stephen Toulmin was a British philosopher who introduced this model in 1958 in his book called '*The Uses of Argument*'. The primary purpose of this model was to analyze arguments for their totality, successful presentation, and effectiveness. However, in later years its elements started being used as a checklist for argumentative writing.

The Toulmin model proposes that an argument should have six parts. The following table tells us what the parts are:

| | |
|---|---|
| Claim | This is the position being taken by the author. It is what the author believes and wants the reader to follow or believe too after reading the argument. This is similar to the thesis statement that we have in the classical model. |
| Evidence | This section of the argument provides the data and statistics that the writer uses to inform the reader about his or her claim. What counts as a valid evidence is expert opinion, survey results and study reports or statistics released by an established authority. They tell the reader why the author is saying what s/he is saying. |
| Warrant | To state the claim and provide information in support of the same is not enough. The reader must be taken through the journey of deduction that the writer went on and help the readers in connecting the dots. Simply put, the warrant links the claim to the evidence through a statement of the assumptions made, understanding achieved and connections established. This is important for the argument to strike a chord with the reader because it is possible that the two parties are on different levels of comprehension and have varying knowledge sources. |
| Backing | The way that evidence supports claims, backing supports warrants. Backing refers to the information provided to establish the warrant as a valid and considerable explanation. It provides further statistics and data to so support the enunciation. |
| Rebuttal | This part of the argument makes the writer consider the most potent opposition points against the stated claim and either concede or agree to the same, refute or deny it or propose a compromise or change to it. Rebuttals, as per Toulmin lend refinement and entirety to an argument. They also give more credence to the writer's position as having been framed post a consideration to opposing perspectives. |
| Qualifiers | These are in a way a defence mechanism that was introduced to protect the author from further rebuttals and counter claims. Use of qualifiers prevents the writer from making sweeping statements and also to lend some degree of certainty to a claim. Examples of qualifiers are words like many, most, possibly, probably, often, etc. |

Toulmin talked about these parts as essential aspects of an argument, however, their position within an argumentative essay is as per norm. So, the claim rests in the introductory paragraph while the evidence, warrants and the backing for the warrants stick together. The rebuttal forms a separate paragraph along with the author's response to the same and a suitable explanation. The qualifiers are mainly seen within the claim and the conclusion.

David Wright created a diagrammatical representation of the Toulmin Model. It is given below. Further down is a demonstrative argument to reflect the six parts of the model.

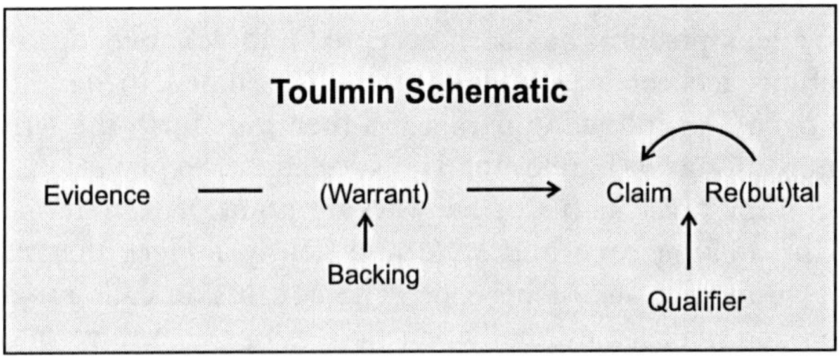


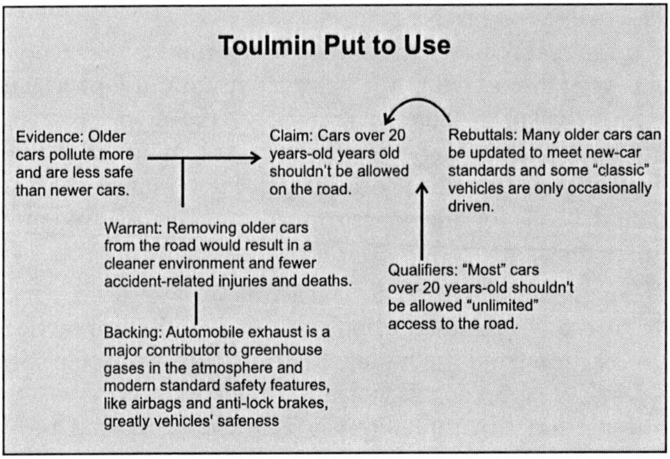


Yet another model for presenting an argument is the Rogerian model proposed by Carl Rogers, a psychologist. Unlike the previous models which have an approach of 'I win you lose', this model looks for a 'common ground' between the reader and the writer and tries to create a 'win-win' feeling for both. The model expects the author to know his or her audience and analyze their position and thoughts on the topic. It believes in gently nudging the readers to accept the writer's position.

In contrast to the introductory paragraphs in the models discussed earlier, the introduction in this model describes the issue and explains the problem. It puts forth the concern as a shared predicament and seeks to establish a connection between the reader and the writer. The first body paragraph presents for consideration, the assumed perspective of the reader and offers to explain the thought process behind the position held. Once the reader's position has been accepted and acknowledged and hopefully accurately explained, s/he is assumed to have been won over. The following paragraph then puts forth the writer's opinion along with relevant statistics, data, explanation, etc. The author presents his or her varying point of view in a very non-threatening tone and style and gently nudges the reader to move over to his or her side. The conclusion calls for joint action and makes a mutually beneficial proposal as a resolution to the problem.

This model requires the author to use mild language and be careful yet fair in laying out perspectives and adopt a neutral tone in articulation. Since a premise of the model is that the author knows the reader closely, it expects him or her to analyze their views and thought processes presented almost accurately. This model calls for allegiance to reason as opposed to emotion and uses the same to draw out a common goal.

Though the above comes across as an approach which is likely to receive minimal opposition, it is quite impractical in its expectation from the author to know the audience in depth. This kind of approach is normally used to express views on highly emotionally charged topics. However, choosing a format for presentation is the writer's prerogative.

The Rogerian model is often confused to be a form of argumentative writing even though the former is very close in its purpose and approach to persuasive writing. However, it differs on account of its consideration of the opposing positions. In persuasive essays the author uses the entire essay to lay out his or her opinions and views on a topic and provides ample and suitable support for the same with a view to persuading the reader to agree and accept the writer's claim to be true and valid.

### 5. *Analytical Essays*

This is an interesting kind of Academic writing which depicts the writer's opinion on the work of another writer, a picture, movie, essay, painting, etc. The process of analysis requires the complex whole to be broken up into its component parts and examined thereafter. The analyst understands the relationship between the different parts and presents his or her understanding in an essay form. Such an endeavour allows the reader to engage with the original form of the text, picture, event, etc. better by having enabled a deeper involvement.

While analyzing an essay the questions considered and addressed by the writer are different from what s/he would look at when analyzing a situation, a book or a movie. However, the primary concerns of an analyst are to understand and explain the following aspects of the subject being explored:

- What is the creator's purpose?
- Who is the target audience?
- What impact does the creator wish to make on the audience?
- Why is it important to create the stated impact?
- Which devices has the creator chosen to make the desired impact?
- Why have these particular devices been used?
- What impact are they likely to create?
- How do the devices work together to create the desired impact?
- How do the various devices work together towards achieving the final goal as set by the creator?

While analyzing a subject, the writer is not stating his or her opinion on what the creator has done, rather it is a discussion on the creator's work and the impression it creates on the author. Before the author starts the analysis, it is important to observe and identify an overall impact that the creation leaves. After this, it is important to acknowledge the main ideas being put across by the creator through his or her work. The approach used here is to move from considering the big picture to studying its component parts, from general to specific. While analyzing the sections of the whole, the writer must decide which aspects of the creation s/he wants to examine. This decision is conveyed through the theme or thesis statement included in the introductory paragraph.

Like all other academic essays, an analytical essay too has an introduction which refers specifically to the work that the author plans to analyze. This introduction includes the title of the work, the creator's name, when it was created and any other detail that must be provided to make the reader comprehend and be well acquainted with the subject being analyzed and to understand the writer's arguments and explanations offered by the writer later in the text. The introduction is a good place to convey to the reader the central theme of the work being analyzed. A factual yet captivating comment on the central theme is a good way to start the introduction in keeping with the principle of general to specific. The paragraph culminates with the thesis statement for the essay. For example,

> "Wars have been known to leave indelible marks on the lives of children of the warring nations. No matter who wins and who loses, the children of all the fighting countries are always at a loss. Deborah Ellis in her book The Breadwinner, first published in year 2000, explores the impact of the Afghan war on the lives of the Afghani women and children. The title of this book refers to the role that the protagonist of the story had to take on as a result of the circumstances in the Taliban era in Afghanistan. This essay analyzes the social and economic impact of the Taliban laws on the lives of the Afghani women and children."

The body paragraphs following the introduction address the criteria of analysis identified in the theme statement one by one. The main idea is put forth by the writer through the topic sentence of the paragraph about one aspect of the creation as mentioned in the thesis statement, followed by an explanation of the writer's understanding and evidence from the creation based on which the stated conclusion as encased in the main idea was drawn. The main idea gives information about the writer's stance on an identified criterion and is supported with evidence from the subject content. The explanation is essentially an analysis of the subject in keeping with the main idea as well as an attempt to establish how the evidence supports the claim.

The conclusion calls for a summarizing of the main arguments discussed in the body paragraphs while linking them to the central theme. The writer essentially establishes how the points raised in the body of the essay relate to the theme projected by the subject. The writer could also go back to the 'big idea' mentioned in the introductory paragraph and seal the essay. It is imperative to note here that no new idea or observation on the subject must be mentioned in the concluding paragraph.

Writing an analytical essay requires the writer to be aware of the intrinsic elements involved in the creation of the subject of analysis. In fact, the writer must not only be aware of the tools of creation but should also understand, where and when these tools are and can be used, what are their limitations and benefits are. He also has to be aware of the impact they create on the audience. The author must comprehend the synergies that the tools share and to what extent they can be used in collaboration to create the desired results. For example, to be adequately equipped to analyze a literary text the writer must be well acquainted with how to form a literary device, how to use it and what effect can be created on the audience with its use. In addition, the writer must also know which literary tool can be used with which literary text. For example, alliteration is a tool mainly used in poetry and not so common in prose. Only when one is aware of the functional significance of the component parts can one analyze the whole.

### 6. *Evaluative Essays*

The evaluative academic essays follow from the analytical essay. Having dissected the parts of a subject, studied and understood the functioning of individual parts in the context of the whole as well as their impact as a unit, it is imperative to state an opinion on the piece so deeply analyzed. This can be done through the process of evaluation. Through an evaluative essay the writer voices his or her opinion on the success of a creative piece in making its desired impression on the target audience as well as on the quality of the creation in general. Evaluation also involves studying other positions on the creation and either agreeing or disagreeing with them. Evaluative writing at the university level also means that the analysis is preceded by the evaluation of the different body paragraphs.

The main purpose of an evaluative essay is to assess a subject based on certain criteria as well as valid evidence in the form of statistics and expert opinion. Other evaluations and accepted facts establish whether the subject has lived up to expectations set with regard to the stated criterion or not. For example, a mystery story can be assessed on its plot, use of the varied literary devices for creating the required setting and milieu and the feeling it leaves the readers with. The writer makes an overall opinion on a subject being evaluated and seeks to convey the same in an apparently unbiased manner using neutral diction and statistical evidence. The absence of bias is important to be put across to effectively appeal to the readers' reason and receive acceptance of the viewpoint.

The introductory paragraph in an evaluative essay gives all relevant information about the subject. It may include information on the current validity of the subject, the importance of the impact the subject creates on the people and the requirement of an evaluation being called for. The introduction also states the overall purpose or goal and establishes the criteria that it will evaluate the subject in. This sets the boundaries within which the essay will operate. The body paragraphs pick up one criterion at a time, state the writer's opinion or judgment on the same to form the topic sentence. Thereafter the author explains his or her claim by pointing out instances from the subject content. The writer also calls upon expert quotes, established theories, statistics, and research data to give credence to his or her claim. Akin to an argumentative essay, here too an objection to the author's stance or opposing views are stated and refuted with the help of suitable evidence. The conclusion sums up the author's claim along with stating an overall position on the subject.

Selecting the set of criteria for evaluating a subject is the most critical part of writing this essay. For every subject, the criteria that might be chosen for evaluation will vary depending on the significance of the subject and the value it adds to the audience's life. For example, a cupboard can be evaluated on its design, capacity, size, shape and maybe even appearance since it is these features that are considered when making a purchase.

A comic movie is expected to make people laugh through its use of sound, expressions and comic timing of the actors and the story line which offers the opportunity to introduce comedy and characterization. It is on the basis of one or more of these criteria that it can be evaluated. Before stating the criteria chosen to evaluate a subject, it makes perfect sense to mention the ideal characteristics and expectation from the subject to be able to decide which yardsticks are the most important to consider. For example, once we state what the expectations from a good hotel are, it becomes easier for the writer to choose the criteria on the basis of which to evaluate a hotel. This information is fundamental as it allows the reader to create an image of the ideal subject and to connect more deeply with the author during the evaluation process.

Judging a subject on the criteria chosen in the thesis statement is the next most important task in an evaluative essay. The author decides whether the subject matches the expectations or not and frames his or her stance on the criterion being considered. Once the stance has been stated the writer must provide evidence in support of the argument to influence the reader to agree with the same.

It is likely that one might confuse between a review and an evaluation. Though they are similar to some extent, yet there are fundamental differences between the two which are important to highlight. While an evaluation analyzes a criterion for an in-depth study, a review offers a more general approach to the assessment. Additionally, while an evaluation must be backed by valid and relevant evidence, a review is essentially the writer's own opinion and does not need support in the form of statistical data or any other. Another important difference is that an evaluation is criterion based while a review is not so. Finally, unlike in an evaluation, no reference to expert opinions or other studies or research reports is required in a review.

An effective evaluation is one that camouflages the writers bias under a carefully chosen neutral tone and expressions in conformity with it and is able to influence the reader to agree with the writer's take on the subject.

## Some Other Types of Response Essays

Other than the ones discussed in detail above, there are some more kinds of essays which are written in academics. Some of these are the cause and effect essay; the opinion essay; advantage-disadvantage essay and the for and against essay. These essays are quite straight forward in their approach and have a simple organization. Let us look at them briefly.

The first kind of essay being discussed here is the cause and effect essay. This kind of essay has a common presence in Academic writing. In this essay, the writer either states an event or describes a situation, action or behaviour and then discusses either causes or the effects of the same in the following paragraphs. They essentially deal with the subject of what happens and why it happens. There are three ways of organizing a cause and effect essay. One, the effect is the point of start and this is mentioned in the introductory paragraph. The body paragraphs discuss the multiple causes of the effect with supporting explanations and evidence. For example, the presence of pollution in the water bodies around us is our effect and in the following part of the essay, the situations which led to it, the causes of the pollution can be discussed. Another is where the initiation point is the cause or a situation, behaviour or action the effect of which is of credence. In this organization approach the situation, behaviour or action is treated as the cause and mentioned in the introductory paragraph. The effects of the same are debated over in the following body paragraphs. For instance, presence of pollution in the air in our environment is a situation. The impact this has on our health, economic situation and maybe social life can be the debate carried on in the essay body. Sometimes there can be multiple causes for an event, situation, behaviour or action and each cause can lead to a different impression or effect. These are discussed in a causal chain format where each paragraph has a different cause and effect described. The conclusion ties all the loose ends together and sums up the overall cause and effect relationship. Sometimes, a solution can be suggested to the perceived problematic situation. There are specific cause and effect transitions that can be used in this essay for signposting to the reader. Transitions like 'as a result', 'consequently', 'for this reason', 'so', 'therefore' can be used to introduce effects while linking phrases like, 'due to', 'one reason for...is', 'one cause is', 'since', 'due to' can be used to introduce a cause. It is important for the writer to be able to appropriately and accurately use such transitions to indicate the movement of thought.

The next kind of writing often used in academic contexts is the opinion essay. As the name suggests, such write-ups are an expression of the author's opinion on a topic. There is explicit mention of what the author believes in through the use of expressions like, 'I believe', 'I think', 'to my mind', etc. The essay can either present a one-sided argument in favour or against the topic of discussion like a persuasive essay or can present both the sides of the debate as in an argumentative essay. The difference lies in the use of personal pronouns and a direct expression of opinion. In this kind of an essay, the opinion of the writer is directly and clearly expressed in the introduction, while the following paragraphs are dedicated to explaining the reasons for the opinion and examples supporting the line of thought. In case the writer wants to include the opposing opinions that might exist for the topic, s/he might so include them along with stating why people might so believe followed by either an acceptance or a denial of the same with reasons. The concluding statement is a summary of the discussion with a paraphrase of the author's opinion.

The 'for and against' as well as the 'advantage-disadvantage' essays follow an identical pattern wherein one argument along with explanations and evidence appears in one paragraph while the opposing argument with the same accompaniments appears in the following paragraph. The introduction in both kinds of essays explains the topic and seeks to bring the reader on the same page as the writer by explaining any concepts or terms that might be interpreted in more than one way. The conclusion in both gives a summary of the discussion and makes a concluding remark.

### Research Essays

A research paper requires the writer to identify a topic, study it in depth to identify a specific gap, make a hypothesis to either explain or fill the gap based on the knowledge currently available, study other research papers that might have been written on the same issue, state what the research says and what it does not along with mentioning whether the isolated gap is explained, filled completely or partially or not at all thus either making a case for further investigation or declaring the initiation null and void. In case of the former, additional exploration can be commenced to achieve desired results.

At the school level, such research writing takes the form of a laboratory report. In the course of a higher study, the same research is expressed through IMRaD or Introduction, Methods, Results, and Discussion method in the form of a full paper. In social science research, studies are presented using the CARS or Creating A Research Space model. A research essay can also be called a problem-solution essay wherein a problem is identified, and extensive research is conducted to find a viable and practical solution to it.

In this book, we are essentially looking to educate school students and teachers in aspects of Academic writing, hence though we have discussed all formats of academically written paper presentations, we will elaborate only those which are relevant to a school situation. In keeping with the stated aim, let us look at the structure and content of a laboratory report.

#### *Laboratory Reports*

The predominant objective of a laboratory report is to record the purpose, procedure and learning derived from an experiment that takes place in a laboratory. Such reports are meant to preserve work done in the diverse fields of Science and document the proceedings for future reference.

It is a well-known and accepted fact that curiosity leads to creation of new knowledge. We observe things happening around us. A logical mind looks for a reason in all happenings. When such a reason is not readily available or the existing explanation does not appeal to the inquiring brain, a hypothesis is assumed, and a procedure is followed to prove it right or wrong. For instance, it is observed that two plants which receive the same sunlight, water, manure, and care grow at different rates. Why is there a difference in the growth rates even when the exposure received is identical? "What factors influence the rate of growth?" can be an inquiry question. For the experiment conducted in this case a laboratory report can be written to chronicle the findings along with the respective success or failure in answering future questions.

The laboratory report, like the other essays starts with an introduction. The introduction describes the context of the experiment and states whatever background knowledge the writer might have regarding the context of the experimental exercise. Essentially, the writer states what s/he seeks to inquire and explains the situation that lead to the arising of the question. Once the question so emerges, the author must commence extensive reading in the same context. This is recommended, as it could be that the question has already been answered. In such a situation, the case for undertaking the experiment dissolves for lack of purpose. It could also be that the author comes upon some useful and important information regarding the case being studied. In this scenario, when the answer to the inquiry has not been found, all the knowledge that the writer already had and the knowledge that s/he has acquired from the research conducted is detailed in the introductory section of the report.

In the next section the author states why it is useful or important to find the answer to the question raised. This explanation lends validity to the experiment and helps it find favour with the readers. For example, if it is known what impacts the rate of growth in plants, it can help environmentalists replenish the lost greenery cover faster and arrest the air quality deterioration. Apart from giving the reasoning behind the experiment, the writer also states a hypothesis based on the overall knowledge that the researcher has so far acquired. This hypothesis is basically an educated guess about what the reason for an action or inaction could be. An outcome is anticipated, and the experiment is conducted to either prove the anticipation correct or incorrect. It is imperative that this hypothesis postulates a cause and effect relationship while stating the supposition at this stage and predicts a particular outcome based on the related model or theory. Care must be taken that the hypothesis stated comes across as a statement of fact which can be tested for its validity and can be proved right or wrong through the process of scientific discovery.

Once the background knowledge has been so delineated, the report moves on to lay down the procedure for the experiment. Before the investigation begins, it is critical for the researcher to identify the independent variables, dependent variables, and the controlled variables while the scrutiny is in process. A variable is any measurable attribute in an experiment that can be changed in quality or quantity across the experiment. There are three kinds of variables in scientific research:

1. **Independent Variable:** These are those variables which are changed or manipulated in quality or quantity by the inquirer in the course of the experiment to study its impact on other variables. When trying to identify the cause of something, we normally focus on one independent variable at a time so as to be able to isolate its impact on the object of study. If there are more than one variable being manoeuvred, it might become difficult to isolate an impact and identify the cause for an effect with certainty. Once one independent variable has been eliminated as being the cause, another factor can be brought in as the independent variable. The same can also be changed in case the inquirer wants to identify more than one reason for the impact or believes that another variable might be more impactful.

2. **Dependent Variable:** The factor which changes in response to the manipulation of the independent variable is the dependent variable. Though there can be multiple factors that might showcase a change in behaviour or appearance as a result of the change introduced in the independent variable, yet in order to arrive at relatively accurate findings, we must focus on only one dependent variable at a time. Once the effect on one dependent variable has been analyzed, the inquirer can move on to studying the response of another dependent variable to the same independent variable or another as required or desired.
3. **Controlled Variable:** These are all the other variables that must be kept stable in order to isolate and highlight the effect created by the independent variable on the dependent variable. For example, if an experiment studies the effect of the amount of sunlight on the rate of growth and uses three potted plants for the same placing one in direct sunlight, another in slight shade and the third in the dark, variables like the variety of plant, amount and quality of soil in each pot, the size of the plant, the size of the pot, amount of water and manure, age of the plant, etc. must be identical or controlled. In the same way if an experiment studies how two chemicals combine at varying degrees of heat, all other factors like the quantity and quality of the chemicals, size of the burner, thickness of the beaker that holds the chemicals, etc. should be kept identical while changing the size of the flame.

Once the three mentioned variables have been identified, the next piece of information sought is the list of materials required for the experiment along with the quantity of each. It is critical to mention very clearly the measuring unit for the quantities and the name of the brand if quality is to differ in the varying brands. This data is followed by a step by step statement of the procedure to be adhered to. It is a good practice to be as detailed and specific as possible here since interpretations might be different. It makes for a good exercise to include pictures of the apparatus and some stages of the experiment in the report. While conducting the experiment, the readings arrived at as a result of the series of identical experiments must be clearly and carefully noted under appropriate and descriptive titles, preferably in an appropriately created or chosen table. This is the raw data that we collect to later analyze and arrive at conclusions either in favour or against the hypothesis. Along with the raw date, any variation from the norm noticed, any problem faced or any restriction experienced should be noted in the form of comments.

The raw data collected is used to analyze the results achieved and deduce the implications of the same while at the same time stating whether the experiment has proved the hypothesis right or wrong. The observations made and readings noted are explained in detail and the reasoning used to state the final claim is to be expounded. While concluding the laboratory report, the author must also evaluate the results against those achieved as a consequence of the experiments conducted regarding the same inquiry earlier, if applicable. The comparison should mention the similarities and discrepancies noted in the set-up of the study as well as the readings achieved. The problems faced in the course of the proceedings and the probable influence of the same on the results arrived at or the data noted must be clearly elucidated too.

This chapter has discussed most of the major response essay types with a view to acquainting the students and teachers in school with the various kinds of writing that they might be called upon to produce and teach respectively. For the students, it is useful as well as critical to understand how a question asking him or her to evaluate, analyze, compare and contrast, etc. is to be addressed. On the other hand, for a teacher it is important to know and understand which areas of a type should be discussed in class and to what length of detail. An effective way to help students produce good quality essays is to brainstorm the essay content in class first. The teacher may choose to use a related topic for this practice exercise rather than the one identified for the assessment. It is also a good idea to elicit what transition phrases or words will be used to perform different functions in the writing. For example, the transition expressions used to add information, to present a contrast or to exemplify. These can be written on the board as the students respond. A better option would be to use a chart paper for noting down the student responses, and later putting the chart up in the class for reference by the pupils. This exercise will draw their attention towards these phrases and may make them use these linking phrases in their write ups. It would also serve to prepare the students well if the organization of the essay were discussed in detail before the actual exercise of writing it is set.

## Works Cited

Bailey, Stephen. "Academic Writing: A Handbook for International Students." Amazon, Routledge, 2018, www.amazon.com/AcademicWriting-Handbook-International-Students/dp/1138048747.

Belcher, Diane, and George Braine, editors. *Academic Writing in a Second Language: Essays on Research and Pedagogy.* Ablex, 1995.

Creme, Phyllis, and Mary R Lea. *Writing at University: A Guide for Students.* McGraw Hill Open University Press, 2008.

Dew, Stephen E. *Academic Writing Skills for ESL Students: Practical English Essay Writing Skills.* Hbicambodia.com, 2013.

Hewings, Martin. *Academic Writing in Context: Implications and Applications.* University of Birmingham Press, 2006.

Hunter, Ian. *Write That Essay: A Practical Guide to Writing Better Essays and Achieving Higher Grades.* McGraw-Hill, 2008.

Jaffe, Charlotte, and Barbara Doherty. *Descriptive Writing with a Purpose.* Educational Impressions, 2007.

Johnson, Andrew P. *Academic Writing: Process and Product.* Rowman & Littlefield, 2016.

Johnson-Farris, Leslie. "Toulmin Model of Argument." *YouTube*, 9 Sept. 2014, www.youtube.com/watch?v=GTd1v6iR97s.

McCarthy, Tara. *Descriptive Writing.* Scholastic Professional Books, 1998.

Raškauskienė, Audronė, et al. *Essay Writing for Exams.* OUP, 2016.

Ravelli, Louise, and Robert A. Ellis, editors. *Analysing Academic Writing: Contextualized Frameworks.* Continuum, 2005.

Starkey, David. *Academic Writing Now: A Brief Guide for Busy Students.* Broadview Press, 2017.

Wood, Nancy V. *Writing Argumentative Essays.* Prentice Hall., 2000.

Wright, David. "The Toulmin Model of Argumentation." *YouTube*, 21 Feb. 2012, www.youtube.com/watch?v=D-YPPQztuOY.

# 6
# Cohesion and Coherence

Cohesion and coherence are innate and indispensable qualities of academic texts, or for that matter any text. While one holds the entire text together, the other creates links within the written piece. Both are necessary to make a written work worthy of consideration and accepted by the target audience as a worthy contribution. Let us look at what each of them means, how each contributes towards a text and the ways in which each can be successfully employed in written articulation. I would like to mention a caveat here that since both coherence and cohesion are topics on which entire books can be written and have been written, I would not be going too deep into either concept in this book which delves into Academic writing as a whole with only the necessary details on inbuilt parts.

## What is Cohesion?

Cohesion refers to the flow or connectedness of a text. It refers to the tying together of ideas, interweaving old or known information with new knowledge in a way that allows the two to combine effortlessly in the mind of the reader who is enabled to enjoy for enhanced comprehensibility. To demonstrate how a text may appear in the absence of cohesion, look at the short paragraph below.

> The hotel is famous. It is one of the most well-known hotels in the country. The latest international dancing competition was held at the hotel. The hotel spent a lot of money to advertise the event. Because the hotel wanted to gain international reputation. But not many

> people attended the event. (https://www.uwb.edu/wacc/what-we-do/eslhandbook/coherence)

Let us now read another version of the above paragraph which is more cohesively written.

> To gain international recognition, one of the most well-known hotels in the country volunteered to host the latest international dancing competition in its premises. Although, the hotel spent a lot of money in advertising the event, not many people attended it and the hotel did not receive the kind of attention it was looking for.

While defining and at the same time laying stress upon the centrality and importance of cohesion in Academic writing, Phyllis Crème and Mary R. Lea stated,

> Cohesion is concerned with the way in which parts of written texts fit together to make a whole rather than a series of disconnected bits.... The connecting devices help to carry your argument along and lend structure to your writing, so that the reader finds it easier to understand.

Halliday and Hasan in their book, *Cohesion in English* mention that it is cohesion that lends 'texture' to a text by establishing 'ties' between the sentences. They say that the concept of cohesion, which refers to the relationship of meaning that exists within a piece of text is semantic, and the very quality that makes a collection of sentences a text. They state that cohesion occurs when the interpretation of some element in the discourse is dependent on that of another. The one presupposes the other, in the sense that it cannot be effectively decoded except by recourse to the concerned other. When this happens, a relationship of cohesion is set up, and the two elements, the presupposing and the presupposed, are thereby, at least potentially, integrated into a text.

Essentially, cohesion knits sentences placed together semantically to create meaningful texts. There are two ways to achieve cohesion, grammatically and lexically. While the use of repetition, reiteration, use of words from the same noun class, etc. are lexical approaches to achieving cohesiveness, use of ellipsis, substitution, conjunctions, and references are grammatical tools to do the same. Let us look at both aspects one by one.

## Grammatical Cohesion

This term refers to cohesion brought about through the use of the grammatical features of language. As identified by Hasan and Halliday, there are four elements that help a writer introduce grammatical cohesion in a text. They are reference, substitution, ellipsis and conjunctions. Let us first understand reference.

## Reference

Reference occurs in a text when one item in it points out to another item, either in another sentence or line in the same text or to an existence outside the text for its interpretation by the reader. For example,

> "Emily reached school late. She was not allowed to enter it."

In this sentence, 'she' refers to Emily and 'it' refers to the school. Every language provides some constituents for reference. In English these are the personal pronouns, demonstrative adverbs and comparatives. The words that make up these segments of language are indications in themselves that something outside the sentence that they occur in is being referred to. Here we must not forget the role of the definite article 'the' which in its purest form is used to refer to a previous occurrence of the specific item being spoken about.

The items being alluded to can either exist within the same text as the referencing tool or outside the text, but in the context of the situation. For instance:

1. The girl had lost her pet and was frantically running around straining her ears to catch a faint whine or bark from it. ('it' refers to the pet in the text)
2. My mother looked at my dress and said, "Umm this doesn't fit you very well. Try this." ('this' refers to another dress or outfit that the mother brought for her

daughter to try. The item of reference does not exist in the text but is present in the context of the situation.)

Such a text reference as indicated in example '1' above is called 'endophoric reference' while example '2' above is an example of situational reference which is also called 'exophoric reference'. Both endophoric and exophoric references carry instructions to the reader to identify the element being referred to in order to make meaning of the current text. Endophoric reference can also be identified as textual referencing and this reference can be to items that have already appeared in the text before, or will appear in the text ahead. The former situation when the reference is to an element that has been introduced to the reader earlier in the text is called 'anaphora'. In a case where the item being referred to is to be introduced to the reader later is called 'cataphora'. An example of cataphoric reference is,

"Here it comes, the much awaited 'dish of the day'." (the reference word 'it' was introduced before the item it was referring to, the 'dish of the day')

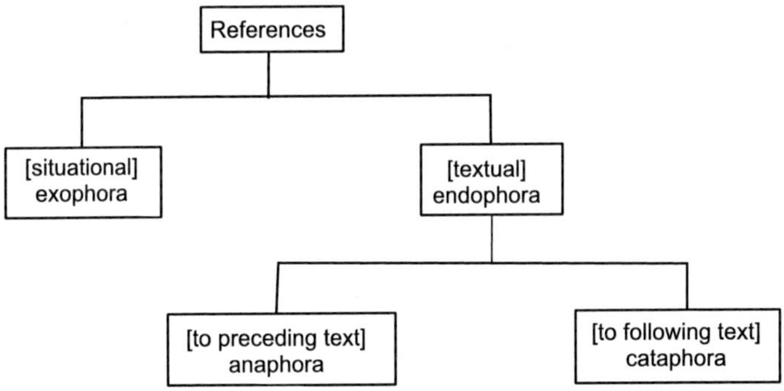


**Fig. 1:** Types of Reference (Halliday & Hasan 1994: 33)

As mentioned earlier, English grammar gives us personal pronouns, demonstrative adverbs and comparative adverbs to help us carry out referencing within texts and contexts. As per Halliday and Hasan (1976), "Personal reference is reference by means of function in the speech situation, through the category of person" (pp. 37-38)

| Semantic category | Existential | Possessive | |
|---|---|---|---|
| Grammatical function | Head | Modifier | |
| Class | Noun (pronoun) | Determiner | |
| *Person:* | | | |
| speaker (only) | I me | Mine | My |
| addressee(s) with/without other person(s) | you | yours | your |
| speaker and other person(s) | we us | ours | our |
| other person, male | he him | his | his |
| other person, female | she her | hers | her |
| other persons; objects | they them | theirs | their |
| object: passage of text | it | [its] | its |
| generalized person | one | | one's |

(Halliday and Hasan, 1976, p. 38)

Personal pronouns that are used for referencing comprise three kinds of pronouns—subjective (I, you, we, they), objective (them, him, her), and possessive (our, mine, their(s)). For example:

> "Tanisha sat on her bed and smirked at me. Her bed was better designed than mine and she knew it."
>
> "I was ready to go to the park with her, but on her bicycle not mine."
>
> "We tried to explain the situation to them but they refused to listen. They just got up from their seats, picked up their bags and walked away."

Apart from personal pronouns, we also have possessive adjectives and possessive pronouns being used for personal referencing. Here the term 'person' is being used to indicate the role of a person in a speech situation. The 'person' reference items are categorized based on the first, second and third person intersecting with the number categories of singular and plural.

"Demonstrative reference is reference by means of location on a scale of proximity." The speaker identifies the demonstrative adjective to be used depending on the proximity of the referent to the speaker.

| *Semantic category* | Selective | | Non-selective |
|---|---|---|---|
| *Grammatical function* | Modifier/Head | Adjunct | Modifier |
| *Class* | determiner | adverb | determiner |
| *Proximity:* | | | |
| near | this these | here [now] | |
| far | that those | there then | |
| neutral | | | the |

(Halliday and Hasan, 1976, p. 38)

Demonstrative adverbs like "this", "that", "those", "these" refer to a location which has either been mentioned earlier or will be introduced later in the text. We also have what we call circumstantial demonstratives like here, now, there and then. They refer to the location of a process or an event and do so directly with no reference to the person or object participating in the process. They appear "extensively with anaphoric function in all varieties of English" (Hasan and Halliday, pp. 59-60).

> "Earlier going for a movie was a family affair. It is different now."
>
> "Today we have computers for everything and in multiple forms. Back then we did everything on our own."
>
> "This", "that", "these" and "those" are called nominal demonstratives. Some instances are:
>
> "This is the city of my birth. Here I learned to dream and it is here again that I fulfilled them. Ladies and gentlemen! Welcome to Mumbai!"
>
> "The party was very boring. Everyone there was busy on their phones and no one wanted to interact."

"Comparative reference is indirect reference by means of identity or similarity". There can be a 'general' or a 'particular' comparison. A 'general comparison' is when all that is being looked at is similarity or distinction between two people, objects, processes or events without respect to any specific property or characteristic. Phrases like 'similar to', 'different from', 'likewise', 'similarly', etc. are used to express such general comparison. Particular comparison on the other hand, refers to an identified quality, feature or characteristic that is compared. It is articulated through expressions like bigger, more beautiful, most intelligent, etc. Both the comparative forms mentioned are referential in nature. The referent may either be present in the text or in the situation. However, like personal reference, this kind of reference also works best with anaphora to build in cohesion in academic contexts.

| *Grammatical functions* | Modifier: Deictic/Epither (see below) | Submodifier/Adjunct |
|---|---|---|
| *Class* | adjective | adverb |
| *General comparison:*<br>identity<br>general similarity<br>difference (*i.e.* non-identity or similarity) | same identical equal<br>similar additional<br>other different else | identically<br>similarly likewise so such<br>differently otherwise |
| *Particular Comparison:* | better, more etc. [comparative adjectives and quantifiers] | so more less equally |

(Halliday and Hasan, 1976, p. 38)

Comparative adverbs are expressions like "heavier", "more intelligent", "bigger", "more comfortable", etc.

Let us observe the following sentences for an illustration.

"This chair is too uncomfortable. I want a more cushioned one."

"I used to work for a bigger organization than this one."

"The movie I watched yesterday was longer, but more entertaining than the one I saw today."

All forms of reference are commonly used in Academic writing and most writers are well aware of pronouns and their usage. Comparative and demonstrative adverbs other than probably, "this", "that", "these" and "those" may need some attention. A premise of using endophoric reference is that both the reader and the writer are aware of the context of the situation, that is, have a shared world outside the text. Considering, that Academic writing assumes an unknown or unfamiliar reader, the scope of use of the mentioned form of reference is limited. The reader can belong to any part of the world hence the context referred to by the writer, even if it is the most common situation, might not be known to the reader. This may impede communication. Another point raised regarding exophoric reference is that since they are not internal to a text, they are more instrumental in weaving in coherence since they do contribute to the textuality of a written piece rather than lead to cohesion in the same. Exophoric reference is much more commonly incorporated in academic texts, considering that the referenced entity is within the text and this makes way for a high comprehensibility of the content. A cataphoric reference is more a feature of creative texts and other non-Academic pieces of writing like advertisements, dialogues, monologues, an introduction or a commentary on a place, person, thing or event, etc. That leaves us with anaphora being the omnipresent reference technique in academic texts.

### Substitution

Substitution as another type of cohesive relation, or cohesive tie, is the process in which one item within a text or discourse is replaced by another (cf. Halliday and Hasan, 1994: 88). To put it simply, repetition of an expression can cause an obstruction to the flow in articulation and therefore lead to difficulties in comprehension. To avoid any such unnecessary repetition, we use the concept of 'substitution' to continue the cohesive journey of thoughts and ideas. Substitution is essentially the practice of replacing words or phrases with fillers. To illustrate, let us look at the following statements.

> "I hope you get married before I do." (*do* is the substituted word)
>
> We could also have said,
>
> "I hope you get married before I get married."

(This is not an incorrect expression. It is just not as smooth as the one above.)

An interesting point to be noted here is that these fillers and the expression that has been replaced are perfectly interchangeable.

> "...as a general rule, the substitute item has the same structural function as that for which it substitutes." (Hassan and Halliday, p. 90)

However, such interchangeability sometimes presupposes that the element being substituted has already been referred to at least once before. For example,

"Joseph's house is small and smelly. He should move to a new one."

"Joseph's one is small and smelly. He should move to a new house."

In the second statement, it is evident that the subject of houses has been broached upon earlier sometime in the conversation and hence this utterance is easily comprehended by the reader or listener.

Substitution is a grammatical function rather than a semantic one. It is also true that the structural function of both the substitute and the element replaced is the same.

There are three types of substitutions each of which corresponds to the type of phrase it substitutes. One type is nominal substitution in which we use 'one' or 'ones' to replace nouns or noun phrases. An example is,

"My school is not very progressive in its approach. I must move to one which is."

('one' here is replacing 'school')

In Academic writing complex sentences are a requirement. Such sentences use a lot of nominal words which comprise nouns and noun phrases. This makes knowledge of nominal substitution imperative among students. Another aspect of this kind of substitution that must be known is that the item and its substituting word may differ in number, singular and plural. However, the noun being so replaced must be a countable noun.

Uncountable nouns have no substitution word or phrase for them. In their case, ellipsis comes into play which we will discuss further on. Another case in which substituting does not work is that of proper nouns.

> "I just saw one John walk away. Is he the one you are looking for?"

In this scene, it is evident that there are more than one Johns in the context. In case, there was only one, we could not have applied substitution.

Other than 'one' and 'ones', we can also use 'the same' as a nominal substitute. The difference lies in the fact that while the former replaces only the noun or noun phrase devoid of any qualification attached to it, the latter substitutes the entire expression.

1.

X: "I would like to order for a breakfast of two fried eggs with sautéed vegetables, a piece of bread and some coffee please."

Y: "I'd like to order the same please."

In the text above, 'the same' replaces the 'breakfast' along with the entire description given along with it—

2.

X: "I'd like to order for a breakfast of two fried eggs with sautéed vegetables, a piece of bread and some coffee please."

Y: "I'd like to order one with the same items please."

In the example above, it is interesting to note that 'one' replaces only 'breakfast'. The writer or the speaker must specify the qualifying information separately.

### Verbal Substitution

'Verbal' is another kind of substitution which is realized through the use of the word 'do' or any one of its grammatical modifications like 'does', 'did', 'doing' and 'done' in English. It replaces an entire verbal group in sentences which comprise verbs and any qualifying information about the verb. This it does often accompanied with 'so' or 'the same'. A verbal substitution generally happens beyond the boundaries of a sentence.

1.

X: "Shall I call for the doctor?"

Y: "Please do."

2.

X: "I have been waiting for a long time now. Have you even started for the venue?"

Y: "Yes, I have done so."

3.

X: "The children have planned this event really well. It would be nice to take some tips on planning from them."

Y: "I will be doing so after the event."

4.

X: "This company has given ESOPs to its employees to retain them."

Y: "I know. We have done the same."

Halliday and Hasan (1976) make a generalization regarding the use of the verbal substitute 'do'. They say that this substitution is more a feature of spoken rather than of written texts. They also state that it is used more often in the British form of English than in the American one. However, it is a common form of substitution used in English language, agreeably, more in its spoken form.

## Clausal Substitution

This is the third kind of substitution that is used as a cohesive device in Academic writing. This is brought into action with the use of the words 'so' and 'not'. Like in the above two types of substitutions, the structural function of this substitution is the same as that of the substituted clause. This replacing element falls last in the progression of replacements. While 'one' replaces just the noun or noun phrase minus the additional information about the noun, 'do' replaces the verb or verb phrase along with the other qualifying information present in the sentence.

In clausal substitution, the entire clause is replaced with either 'so' or 'not'.

1.

X: "Have they gone home?"

Y: "I believe so."

2.

X: "Have they gone home?"

Y: "I believe not."

However, sometimes while substituting a negative verb, the negation takes into account the normally used negative form of the verb in the clause. For instance;

X: "I think they believe we are at fault."

Y: "I don't think so."

In the example above, instead of saying "I think not", it is more appropriate to say, "I don't think so". This happens very commonly when using words like 'believe', 'suppose', 'imagine', etc. Substitution is a common practice when making impersonal comments. For example,

X: "Should we follow the rule book to the last word?"

Y: "They say so."

Here 'they' is not anyone known but the general public who may or may not be associated with the context.

There are three kinds of clauses that are replaced by this type of substitution; reported clause, conditional clause and modal clause. Each of these clauses can either communicate a positive expression or a negative one. To replace the positive articulation, we use 'so' and for the negative, we use 'not'.

X: "I have always been by your side. Isn't it?"

Y: "I believe so."

Here 'so' substitutes 'that you have been by my side'. The 'report' aspect comes from the use of 'that'. This is not a case of reported speech as we understand it where a person is reporting an event, something said or what one saw, etc. to a third person. In reported clause only the declarative statements can be substituted. The imperative and the interrogative reported clauses have no substitute. It is for this reason that clauses which fall after words like 'wonder', 'order' or 'ask' are never substituted.

In conditional expressions, the clause after 'if' is commonly substituted with either 'so' or 'not'. This also applies when a condition is expressed using 'assume' or 'suppose'.

"The share market is likely to crash after the announcement of the budget. If so, we must sell our shares before the budget comes."

1.

X: "The judge is believed to be biased in this case."

Y: "Suppose not, still we have no evidence to prove his innocence."

2.

X: "I think I will pass the exam with flying colours."

Y: "Assuming so, which specialization stream do you plan to choose?"

Explaining modality, Halliday and Hasan (1976, p. 135) say that modality is the speaker's assessment of the probabilities inherent in the situation of the conversation or in a derived sense of rights and duties. We can either use the modal verbs like can, could, will, might, etc. to express modality or modal adverbs like perhaps, probably, possibly, etc. The latter are often followed by a substitute. Talking about the restrictions on the use of substitution in expressing certainty as well as modality, Halliday and Hasan (1976, p. 133) say that though the modals expressing certainty take a substituting expression in the negative, they do not in the positive. Hence, we can say "I'm afraid not", we cannot say "I'm sure so". Similarly, we have restrictions in the use of substitution while expressing modality. We can say "perhaps so" but not "certainly so".

### Ellipsis

Ellipsis is the omission of elements from a spoken text, which are otherwise required by grammar. These elements are omitted on the assumption that they are evident in the context and are well understood by the listener and hence need not be expressed. Though not all that is omitted from a speech is ellipsis, yet it is true that every conversation takes some inputs from the context. Ellipsis as distinguished from other reasons in which parts of a conversation may have been left unsaid refers to 'missing' elements in structure.

X: "Have you asked the children to carry a torch for the camp?"

Y: "I have."

Here the speaker has omitted saying, "asked the children to carry a torch for the camp".

Ellipsis, like substitution, is nominal, verbal and clausal. Nominal ellipsis refers to the omission of the main noun. For example,

"Though I bought the red carpet, I liked the blue better."

In this sentence the main noun, 'carpet' has been omitted since it is evident from the context that it is being referred to in the second part as well.

Another kind of ellipsis is verbal ellipsis, in which the verb or a verb phrase is elliptic. For example,

"Sam has been cheating in class, and Susan too."

In this sentence, 'has been cheating has been left out.'

The last kind of ellipsis is clausal. In this case, an entire clause is omitted. For instance,

X: "Have you ever been to Bora Bora?"

Y: "I have."

In the above example, the entire clause, 'been to Bora Bora' is omitted.

Ellipsis and substitution are both structural approaches to articulation and primarily apply to spoken language, but not so much to written.

> "Ellipsis and substitution assume a lot from the context; they proceed on the basis that omitted and substituted elements are easily recoverable and are therefore natural

> in speech situations where a high degree of contextual support is available (McCarthy, p. 46).

Such contexts are neither available nor considered in Academic writing scenarios. Academic writing requires the author to write as succinctly and precisely as possible with no omissions which assume known or common situations considering that the reader and the writer share a highly distant and formal relationship.

Ellipsis and substitution were discussed for the purpose of presenting a well-rounded discourse on the topic.

## Conjunctions

Though conjunctions do not fall in the same league as reference, ellipsis and substitution, yet they are considered as grammatical cohesive devices. They weave in cohesion through the specific meanings they carry. They do not refer to any presupposed item in the text, mentioned either ahead of them or after them. However, they do assume a textual sequence and signal a relationship between the elements they conjunct.

The conjunctive relationship established in a writing can be achieved in a variety of ways. There is no set or predetermined pattern for the use of conjunctions in Academic writing. Additionally, such a relationship between the elements being combined can be established through the use of a one-word conjunction, a phrasal or a clausal one. For example,

> "They fought over money. *As a result,* there was a lot of bad blood between them."
>
> "The *result* of them fighting over money was a lot of bad blood between them."
>
> "*As a result of them fighting over money*, there was a lot of bad blood between them."

Another aspect of the same quality is that the same relationship can be established using a variety of conjunctive expressions. For example,

> "The baby slept in spite of all the noise around him."
>
> "Although, there was a lot of noise around him, the baby slept."

> "There was a lot of noise around him. Nevertheless, the baby slept."
>
> "Despite all the noise around him, the baby slept."

Hasan and Halliday, explaining this concept say,

> There is a range of different structural guises in which the relations we are calling conjunctive may appear. These relations constitute a highly generalized component within the semantic system, with reflexes spread throughout the language, taking various forms; and their cohesive potential derives from this source. (1976, p. 227)

In Academic writing, a conjunctive association between elements can be established through adverbs, compound adverbs and prepositional phrases, as established by Halliday and Hassan (1976). Adverbs would include words like 'so', 'but', 'because', 'and', 'yet', 'or', 'next', etc. Compound adverbs would be expressions like 'furthermore', 'subsequently', 'therefore', 'henceforth', 'nevertheless', etc. Prepositional phrases would include 'as a result', 'in spite of', 'because of that', 'instead of this', etc.

In most cases, the prepositional phrases appear at the start of the sentence. However, the mentioned terms might appear in any part of the sentence but their impact is observed on the meaning conveyed by the entire articulation unless there is a repudiation, which means setting a limit to the domain of influence. Such restriction on the area of influence is also often placed through the use of a conjunction.

Discussing the types of conjunctions, Halliday and Hasan introduce us to four categories of conjunctions. These are additive, adversative, causal and temporal. To illustrate,

> "The men climbed the mountain at a steady pace and took breaks only when absolutely necessary." (additive)
>
> "The men climbed the mountains at a steady pace yet were unable to reach before dark." (adversative)
>
> "The men climbed the mountain at a steady pace because they wanted to reach the top before sunset." (causal)

> "The mean wanted to reach the mountain top and then hoist their national flag there." (temporal)

The following table which they created (pp. 242-43) demonstrates their classification even more clearly. In the table below, the conjunctions have been classified as establishing an external or an internal relationship between elements. The relationship is external when the conjunction makes the addition, causality, adversity as well as temporality evident by using specific conjunctions. The same is internal when the relationship of one of the four kinds of conjunctions stated above is internal to the conversation and is assumed or understood by the listener unless specified otherwise. For example,

> "The lady was not treated well by her in-law family, so she left their house at the first opportunity." (external)
>
> "The lady believed life could be better, so she decided to do something about it and left the house at the first opportunity." (internal)

In the second sentence, the speaker or writer has not clearly stated the cause of the lady's leaving. That she was unhappy with the current state of affairs is evident from the language used. Hence the causal relationship is implicit in the expression and therefore internal to the communication. On the other hand, in the first sentence the cause and the result are clearly mentioned. The relationship is explicit in the language.

| | External/Internal | Internal (unless otherwise specified) | | |
|---|---|---|---|---|
| Additive | Additive, simple:<br>Additive *and, and also*<br>Negative *nor, and . . . not*<br>Alternative *or, or else* | Complex, emphatic:<br>Additive *furthermore, in addition, besides*<br>Alternative *alternatively*<br>Complex, de-emphatic:<br>Afterthought *incidentally, by the way* | Apposition:<br>Expository *that is, I mean, in other words*<br>Exemplificatory *for instance, thus* | Comparison:<br>Similar *likewise, similarly, in the same way*<br>Dissimilar *on the other hand, by contrast* |
| Adversative | Adversative 'proper'<br>Simple *yet, though, only*<br>Containing 'and' *but*<br>Emphatic *however, nevertheless, despite this* | Contrastive:<br>Avowal *in fact, actually, as a mater of fact*<br>Contrastive (external):<br>Simple *but, and*<br>Emphatic *however, on the other hand, at the same time* | Correction:<br>Of meaning *instead, rather, on the* ***contrary***<br>Of wording *at least, rather, I mean* | Dismissal:<br>Closed *in any case, in either case, whichever way it is*<br>Exemplificatory *in any case, anyhow, at any rate, however it is* |

(Hasan and Halliday, pp. 242-43)

| | External/Internal | Internal (unless otherwise specified) | | |
|---|---|---|---|---|
| Causal | Causal, general:<br>Simple *so, then, hence, therefore*<br>Emphatic *consequently, because of this*<br>Causal, specific:<br>Reason *for this reason, on account of this*<br>Result *as a result, in consequence*<br>Purpose *for this purpose, with this in mind* | Reversed causal:<br>Simple *for, because*<br>Causal, specific:<br>Reason *it follows, on this basis*<br>Result *arising out of this*<br>Purpose *to this end* | Conditional (also external):<br>Simple *then*<br>Emphatic *in that case, in such an event, that being so*<br>Generalized *under the circumstances*<br>Reversed polarity *otherwise, under other circumstances* | Respective:<br>Direct *in this respect, in this regard, with reference to this*<br>Reversed polarity *otherwise, in other respects, aside from this* |
| Temporal | Temporal, simple (external only):<br>Sequential *then, next, after that*<br>Simul-taneous *just then, at the same time*<br>Proceding *previously, before that*<br>Conclusive:<br>Simple *Finally, at last*<br>Correlative Sequential *first...than at first...*<br>Conclu-sive *in the end* | Complex (external only):<br>Immediate *at once,*<br>Interrupted *thereupon*<br>Repetitive *soon, after a time*<br>Specific *next time,*<br>Durative *on another occasion*<br>Terminal *next day, an hour later*<br>Punctiliar *meanwhile until then at this moment* | Internal temporal:<br>Sequential *then, next, secondly*<br>Conclusive *finally, in conclusion*<br>Correlative forms:<br>Sequential *first...next*<br>Conclusive *...finally* | 'Here and now':<br>Past *up to now, hitherto*<br>Present *at this point, here*<br>Future *from now on, hence-forward*<br>Summary:<br>Sum-marizing *to next up, in short, briefly*<br>Resumpet-ive *to resume, to return to the point* |

# 7
# Teaching Academic Writing

This chapter is the culmination of all the earlier chapters. The study of cohesion and coherence, features of Academic writing and types of academic texts were all discussed to help students as well as teachers understand how Academic writing is different from other forms of writing, and to learn about the varied forms of academic texts that exist and how the language used in these texts varies from that employed in non-academic scenarios. Having introduced and deliberated upon all issues that are imperative to learning and articulation in academic situations in detail, we finally come to considering how all the previous information can be put into practice while writing in academic situations.

Before moving on, let us look at what the multiple texts students in schools might write in their academic surroundings are. Some of these could be annotations to read texts, notes to each other, emails to teachers, response essays, researched essays, laboratory reports, observation notes, class notes, invitations to parents or teachers or both for an occasion and introductory write-ups for events. Apart from these there can be other forms of writing that they may be called upon to do as a part of their schooling. However, not all are 'academic' in nature. Only those kinds of writing that are undertaken as a part of the process of teaching and learning can truly be termed as Academic writing. Considering that in school children are being primarily trained to meet the needs of college and further study related endeavours as far as writing is concerned, we will not regard pieces of writing like annotation, class notes, etc. as academic even though their purpose is the same. This is because they are for one's own consumption and do not share their register with the study texts that we are contemplating. We will essentially scrutinize the teaching of writing in the context of response essays, researched essays, and laboratory reports.

While we consider the teaching of a concept of skill it is important to identify the areas which need attention. This brings us to the gaps in knowledge that make explicit teaching of writing absolutely necessary. Let us look at the mind map below through which some of the common problems with the Academic writing of students in international schools have been outlined.

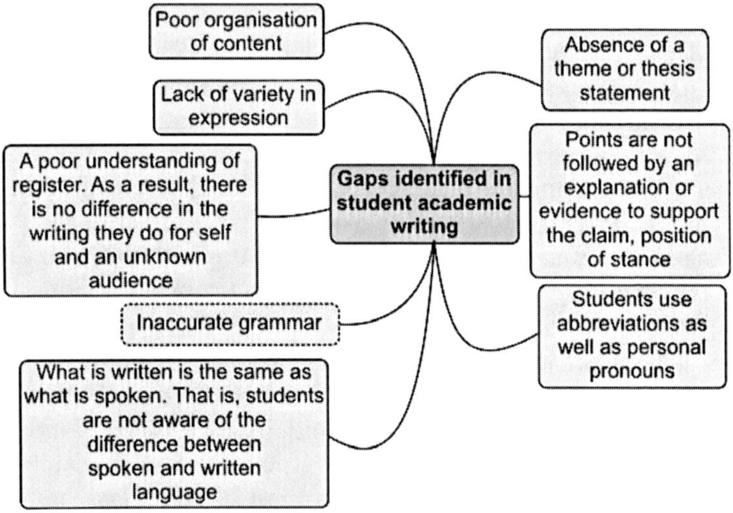


Dealing with these lapses must be done systematically and must be spread over years.

An unfortunate development in English teaching in International schools in countries that do not speak English as the first language is the lack of consistent focus on English grammar. There is so much stress on learning by activity, learner engagement and involvement, and associated strategies that concentration on the bare necessities get side-lined. Since English has been recognized as the lingua franca of the world, International schools use English as the medium of instruction and the comprehension of English language on the part of the students is assumed. Though initial grammar is taught in the primary classes, the continuation of the same in secondary classes is assumed to build up on the basis of the leisure as well as the academic reading the children are expected to do and the English that they are exposed to in their environment. Such language development may happen in many cases. However, there are many instances where this does not happen due to various reasons including family background, excessive distractions in the contexts and interest of the child in language learning per se. Overcoming such impediments calls for careful planning towards facilitating acquisition of Academic language leading to proficiency in Academic writing.

The most important step that must be initiated in schools to promote an understanding and acquisition of Academic English is that the teachers imparting knowledge to the students must practice using the same in their classrooms while they teach or instruct. This leads us to the question, "Do most schoolteachers know the difference between academic and colloquial English?". In more cases the answer will be a 'no'. Such a scenario clearly exhibits the need for educating the teachers in the features of Academic language, its contexts of use as well as how it is different from the language we use to speak. Thus, we bring home the importance of using full forms, an awareness of the slangs that we use in our daily speaking along with the fact that they must be avoided and an understanding of what is going wrong in their classroom language that needs to be mended. An effort to use Academic language while teaching and instructing must be accompanied by constant self-vigilance and careful planning in the beginning and continued till the use of the same becomes a habit.

Once the teachers are trained, the task of teaching Academic language to the students becomes much easier. To expose their students to basic Academic language, teachers could place the common classroom conversations as displays which the students might look at in their free time or as they are looking around the classroom and allow for peripheral learning.

Another way in which teachers could make a seminal contribution towards development of Academic writing skills is by encouraging the practice of backing up claims or positions expressed on varied topics during an orchestrated discussion, an activity or a general conversation with an explanation of the stance along with delineating the thought process which led to such a viewpoint. The students could also be further prompted to state evidences in support of the stated perspective in the form of statistics, observations or opinions and views of experts on the topic. Basically, the students should be encouraged to identify and present reasons for what they believe or feel about a topic. Continuous perpetuation of this practice will establish it as a skill in the student and will help him or her in writing effective response as well as researched essays. When the need for justifying their claims in Academic writing assignments and research work is highlighted, students might find it easier to follow the norm since they have already been practising doing the same in class.

Being able to organize a paragraph as well as a longer text comprising multiple paragraphs are a skill that students need to cultivate. For this they must understand the concept of flow, coherence as well as cohesion. This requirement calls for the establishment and reiteration of the fact that writing is a means of communicating with other people. The major difference between Academic writing and speaking is that the recipient is either someone who shares a highly formal relationship with the writer or is unknown. Moreover, in case the receiver of the communication does not understand or has doubts on a point made in the writing, he or she can seldom approach the writer to seek a clarification. Hence it is the responsibility of the writer to be as concise, clear, and precise as possible to establish an effective transmission between himself/herself and the reader.

A variety of strategies could be used to teach organization of ideas in a paragraph. The following are a few of them:

1. Take the sample of a well-crafted paragraph. One could write one oneself or adopt one from an authentic source or a source created for the purpose of teaching.

The sentences of the paragraph can be separated by cutting them up. Make pairs or groups. Give the cut-up sentences of the paragraph to the student groups to let them use their judgment to recreate the paragraph.

2. Introduce one or two extra lines which are not associated with the point being made in the topic sentence but are related to the topic in the paragraph. Ask the students to identify the unrelated sentences.
3. Make groups of 4 or 5. One student in the group write the topic sentence and passes the sheet of paper or an electronic device to the next student in the group to add the next line. Their task is to write a paragraph with a clear start and a close by each student adding just one line.
4. Students are given two instances of the same paragraph. One is a good example while the other is not. They have to choose one and give reasons for their choice.

It is assumed that these activities will be used only after the teacher has established the structure of a paragraph, has dealt with its component parts extensively and has discussed in detail the use of transition expressions and other cohesive devices which can be used to express the content cohesively and effectively. Once these aspects have been taught, the teacher can simply elicit the relevant expressions that could be used for a given topic and context and write them on the board or on a chart paper before setting up one of the above given or any other activity which will provide an opportunity to use the noted and displayed expressions. Once students understand how a paragraph is written, it is easier to help them establish flow in their long essays. What they need help with now are ways to connect one paragraph to the next in the essay. Accentuating the role of linking expressions can be of much help in this direction. The seminal importance of the theme statement as well as the concluding paragraph must also be emphasized, and efforts must be made to teach the writing of these two important components of Academic essays.

Helping students to build in variety in their language calls for some more action on the part of the teacher. While planning the teacher can identify the sentences, phrases, or words she will work with on a given day. Once so identified, after saying or writing these sentences, phrases, or words the teacher can elicit from the students, other ways of saying the same thing without a drastic change in the meaning. The teacher could encourage looking up synonyms of words, especially adjectives, and discuss the same through the lens of usage in formal or informal contexts, collocations, and the nuances of difference in meaning. This is because a word may be a synonym of another in one context but not so in another. For example, 'pinnacle' has been suggested as a synonym of 'highlight'. However, they are synonyms as nouns not as verbs. The students must be trained to note such facts and then use the synonyms. In fact, the teacher can zero in on certain words which are often used in an academic context, e.g. "focus", make a mind map with the synonyms which can be used in the same context on a chart paper and put it up as a classroom display. The teacher can choose to make the map himself or herself or ask the students to do so. The latter makes way for academic engagement in the activity for the students and they might opt to use the variants more readily.

Normally, curriculums do not devote much time to the teaching of register and style even though an understanding of these is crucial to acquiring Academic writing skills. It is imperative that the teacher set out some time dedicated to these areas of study that might go a long way in helping students become comfortable with the kind of language that is required in the field. The students must be made aware of the different types of registers and the accompanying style to make sense of the entire concept of Academic language and its features. This will hasten the process of Academic language acquisition.

Now that all the probable lapses in the Academic writing mentioned above have been addressed, let us look at the two approaches that teachers can choose from to explicitly teach Academic writing. Here it is plausible to assume that the children have been exposed to and been given a good understanding of register, style, organization of content, ways to vary expression, etc. before this step. Only once the above-mentioned aspects have been dealt with can we move on to taking an overall approach to teaching writing.

There are two approaches to teaching writing. One is the Process approach and the other is the Product approach. Let us discuss the Process approach first.

### The Process Approach to Teaching Writing

Students who are not very confident of their English skills are uncomfortable in writing in the stated language, whether it is for taking down notes as the teacher delivers a lecture, annotating or assessing. This fear can be dealt with by adopting the process approach to teaching writing. The main purpose of instituting this approach in the 1980s was to support the students whose first language was different from the language of the text being written, to overcome their fear of composition in a foreign language wherein their proficiency was limited. Talking about this method, Nunan (1991) says,

> In this approach, the focus in the first instance is on the quantity rather than quality, and beginner writers are encouraged to get their ideas on paper in any shape or form without worrying too much about formal correctness. The approach also encourages collaborative group work between learners as a way of enhancing motivation and developing positive attitudes towards writing. In addition, and more controversially, attention to grammar is played down. (p. 87)

Given that obsession with correctness of grammar can be a huge hurdle to developing fluency and other related language skills, this method of teaching writing is a route to rescue one from the shackles of grammar for the teaching and learning of English writing.

In this method of teaching the students and the teacher go through the process of producing a piece of text together. Students plan, write drafts, receive feedback, edit as per the feedback and rewrite individually or in small groups while the teacher facilitates as well as provides inputs where required.

This cycle is recursive and can continue more than once till the parties involved are satisfied with their creation. Students get time to discuss their ideas, thoughts and opinions and are able to think and about their content as well as the organization and presentation of the same with other students or the teacher, depending on whether they are working in groups or alone. If students work in groups, the process also facilitates peer learning along with acquiring knowledge from a more informed adult, the teacher.

The process writing approach presumes that a writer produces a text for an authentic purpose. Hence the starting point here is the establishing of a situation that demands a written response. The situation must be one that the student(s) is familiar with and has observed its presence in his or her environment, actively or passively. The process starts with a stress on fluency whereby student(s) and the teacher plan the content of the piece, keeping in view its purpose and the audience. Then comes the exercise of arranging the content depending on the structural requirements laid out for the text. These requirements are in keeping with the fact that every kind of text, be it an essay, a letter, a story or any other, has a pre-defined structure which dictates the framework of its content. Since we are only concerned with academic texts here, organization of content primarily refers to planning of the introduction and the conclusion. It also means planning of the paragraphs for an essay or sections in case of reports. Having brainstormed these two aspects of a text, the first draft is written. It is considered for feedback on the matter as well as on its lay out. This feedback can come from oneself, a peer, or a teacher. The text is edited in response to the feedback and a second draft produced. In case the writer and others involved are not satisfied with the final outcome, the cycle of feedback, editing and rewriting is repeated till the product is appreciated by all concerned and considered an effective model of its kind.

Then comes the final action of the process which pushes the writer towards ensuring accuracy in the piece. The text is analysed and scrutinized for its correctness in grammar, spelling and punctuation as well as in its variety and appropriateness in diction. Though the journey undertaken towards producing a text is of utmost importance, the product which results is equally crucial. In fact, the process continues till a satisfactory product emerges as the final draft.

Harmer's (2004) process wheel presents the stages of the writing approach being considered here beautifully. Through his wheel he shows the many directions that the writers can take while still in the process. The writer can move along the rim or go up and down the wheel's spokes. He goes on to say that only when the final version is the final version, is the process considered to have reached its culmination.

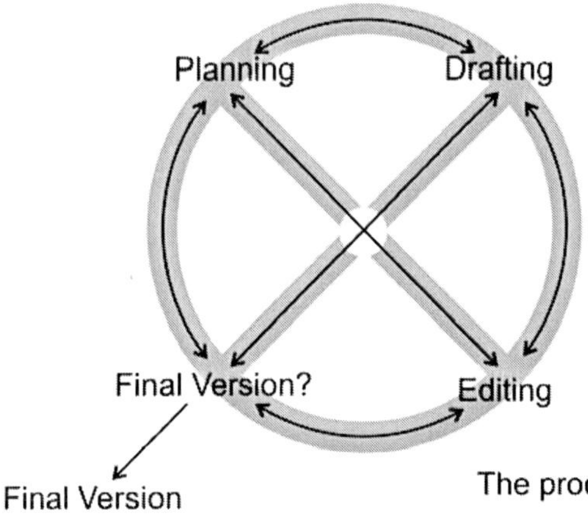


The process wheel

(How to Teach Writing, 2004, p. 6)

Primarily the writing process involves four stages. The first one is planning which is also called the pre-writing stage. Then comes the stage where the students write the first draft. Following this is the stage of revision and editing based on feedback received. Finally, the last draft is written. This may or may not be the final draft. It is a good practice to take the students through each of these stages at least three times. Once for fluency, once for form and finally for accuracy. There could be more occurrences of the cycle depending on the quality of action and the satisfaction with the product arrived at, at the end of a cycle. Let us discuss each stage in detail.

## 1. Planning or pre-writing

This is the most important stage in the process of writing. It is at this juncture that the student's creativity is stimulated, and all previous knowledge related to the topic and the task is invoked. This is primarily a teacher led session where the teacher works towards the above stated goals along with helping the students overcome their fear of written production. This fear might arise from a lack of adequate previous exposure to Academic writing situations. Reading and writing go hand in hand as the former feeds the latter. However, with the unprecedented exposure the students have to electronic media, reading has been relegated to the background in their daily schedules. Through the exposure to international, primarily English, movies, serials and music, children do learn to speak English, but that is the colloquial version of the language not the academic. While they are exposed to written English on the social media, it is not academic. Their exposure to English in academic contexts is limited to their textbooks which again are now just one of the resources used for study not the only. In fact, they are a source of knowledge that are minimally referred to, given that there are much more attractive and interactive modes of learning available. As a result, when it comes to writing in academic contexts, students develop cold feet as it is a less explored territory for them except in case of an assessment. Note-taking is also a rare activity as all resources are shared with the students and annotation is not a common practice. It is of prime importance that the panic arising from situations as mentioned above be dealt with first and effectively so.

An interesting way to help students deal with such fear of Academic writing as mentioned previously is to practice 'free writing'. This technique entails identifying a topic and giving the students a set time period to write anything and everything that come to their mind. They are not allowed to stop writing before the allotted time ends nor lift their writing device, possibly a pen or a pencil. This means even if they are struggling with content at any time during the free writing activity and thinking, "now what should I write I cannot think of anything else." They must write this as well. Regular use of this activity will alleviate the fear of writing to a large extent and they will also develop considerable fluency in the activity. Given the benefits of this task, it should be repeated at regular intervals and students could be encouraged to map their progress in terms of the quality of the content produced under the pressure of time. Such reflection will increase their motivation levels as well as confidence.

Though the above-mentioned activity can be used as a general enterprise to improve writing skills, it can also be used as a part of a focused and task-based writing exercise. A free writing activity on a given topic will help the students to orientate their attention on the topic at hand as well as help them create a mental schema of the subject they are to write on.

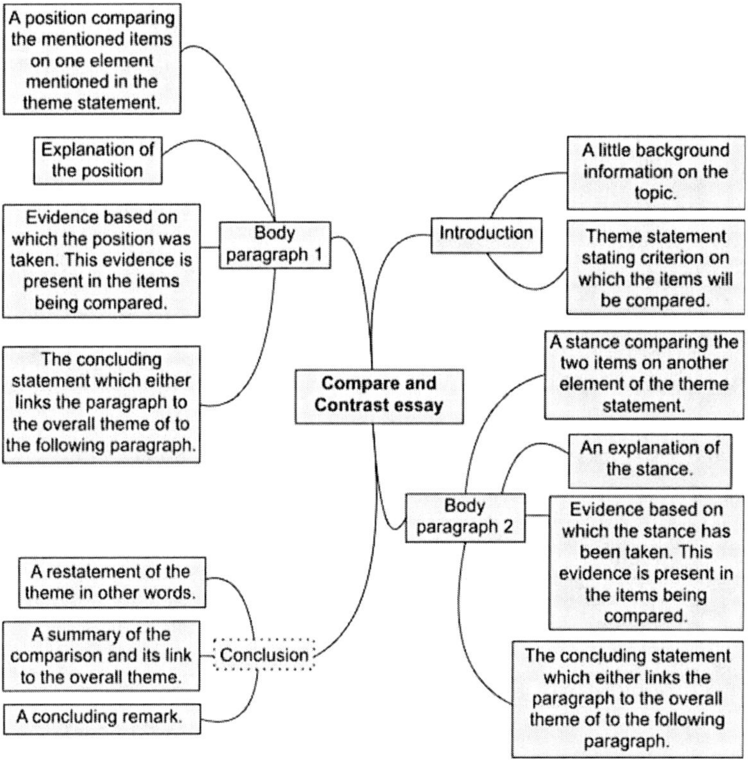


Further to this action, the teacher must discuss the structure of the text type to be written. It is important to draw the students'

attention to the important structural features of the text to be written so that they can be considered and included in the draft.

Let us take the example of a compare and contrast essay for our discussions here. Keeping the above-mentioned text type in mind, the teacher must elicit the structure that the essay has to follow. It must be noted, however, that elicitation can only happen for content that has already been discussed with the students at an earlier instance. Hence, it is assumed that deliberations on the structural characteristics of the various academic text types or in this case that of a compare and contrast essay have been conducted previously. The teacher must elicit from the students the names of the different parts of the essay, namely, the introduction, body paragraphs and the conclusion. He or she must continue to elicit the component parts of each of the parts identified. The information so gathered could be presented on the board in the form of a mind map or could be placed on a chart paper to be put up as a classroom display for future reference.

The mind map given below shows the summary of a discussion that is assumed to have happened in a classroom while planning for a compare and contrast essay.

The above mind map discusses the elements to be included in the essay. Once this has been achieved, the students can start working on the content which depends on the subject of study and the topic of consideration within that subject.

This process can be carried out in two ways. One, the teacher leads the session and elicits what information goes into each part of the essay, as is mentioned in the mind map above. The other, the teacher makes groups of students and hands them copies of a mind map with guiding questions or instructions by answering which the students arrive at the structure of the essay. These guiding questions can be straightforward 'W/H' questions or an activity.

This is a simple guiding structure with W/H questions which pushes the student groups to recall previously imparted information and recollect the structure associated with the text type they need to produce.

While conducting an activity, the teacher can build in some W/H questions along with some multiple-choice questions or a matching activity. The answers to these activities are in most cases quite apparent since the purpose is to guide the students to recollect through engagement rather than be challenged.

This exercise guides the students to remember which part includes what and at the same time engages them by making them choose.

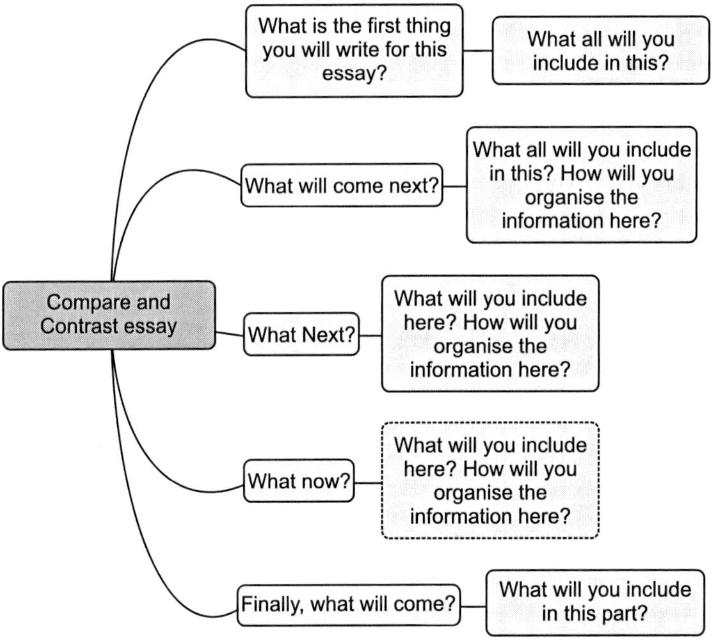


While using the latter method of revising the structure the teacher can build in a bit of differentiation for effectual learning. To put differentiation into play, it is of critical importance to put great thought into the creation of groups for effective functioning and positive results since an important purpose of group work is to allow for peer learning and support to the weaker students in a mixed ability classroom. Although it must be highlighted that thoughtful grouping is seminal to efficacious learning in every case including that of constructive differentiation.

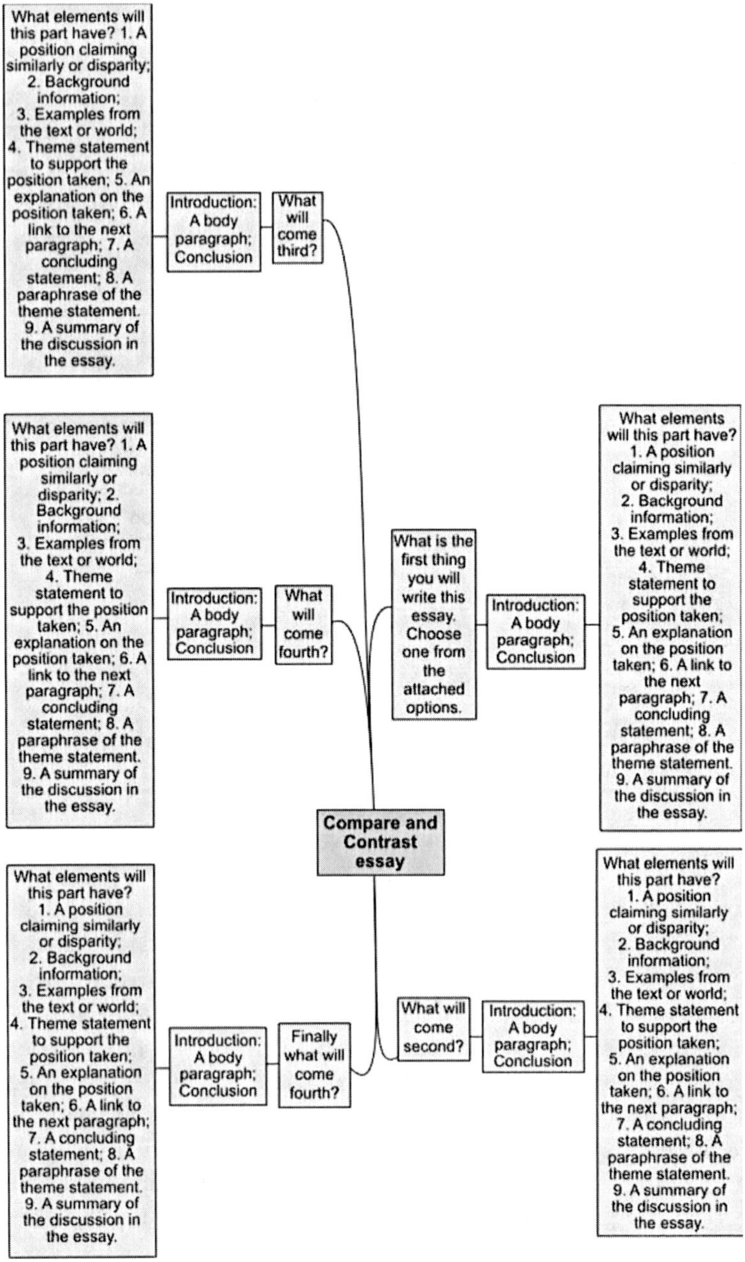
Compare and Contrast essay
What is the first thing you will write this essay. Choose one from the attached options.
Introduction: A body paragraph; Conclusion
What elements will this part have? 1. A position claiming similarly or disparity; 2. Background information; 3. Examples from the text or world; 4. Theme statement to support the position taken; 5. An explanation on the position taken; 6. A link to the next paragraph; 7. A concluding statement; 8. A paraphrase of the theme statement. 9. A summary of the discussion in the essay.
What will come second?
Introduction: A body paragraph; Conclusion
What elements will this part have? 1. A position claiming similarly or disparity; 2. Background information; 3. Examples from the text or world; 4. Theme statement to support the position taken; 5. An explanation on the position taken; 6. A link to the next paragraph; 7. A concluding statement; 8. A paraphrase of the theme statement. 9. A summary of the discussion in the essay.
What will come third?
Introduction: A body paragraph; Conclusion
What elements will this part have? 1. A position claiming similarly or disparity; 2. Background information; 3. Examples from the text or world; 4. Theme statement to support the position taken; 5. An explanation on the position taken; 6. A link to the next paragraph; 7. A concluding statement; 8. A paraphrase of the theme statement. 9. A summary of the discussion in the essay.
What will come fourth?
Introduction: A body paragraph; Conclusion
What elements will this part have? 1. A position claiming similarly or disparity; 2. Background information; 3. Examples from the text or world; 4. Theme statement to support the position taken; 5. An explanation on the position taken; 6. A link to the next paragraph; 7. A concluding statement; 8. A paraphrase of the theme statement. 9. A summary of the discussion in the essay.
Finally what will come fourth?
Introduction: A body paragraph; Conclusion
What elements will this part have? 1. A position claiming similarly or disparity; 2. Background information; 3. Examples from the text or world; 4. Theme statement to support the position taken; 5. An explanation on the position taken; 6. A link to the next paragraph; 7. A concluding statement; 8. A paraphrase of the theme statement. 9. A summary of the discussion in the essay.

As mentioned in the previous paragraph, groups can figure out the structure of an essay either by answering simple W/H questions (refer to the diagram above) or by way of an activity. In the former case, the teacher must make mixed potential groups which has students who are high ability learners, mediocre ability learners and may be some low ability learners. In this group, the high capability learners will automatically take the lead and will take their group through the task with some support from the mediocre learners. The low capability learners will listen and grasp as they receive a repeat exposure to what has been discussed earlier. In the latter case, the groups must consist of similar capability students to enable differentiation practices and to facilitate learning. A set of three activities must be developed which must increase in their level of complexity from one to three, with the first activity being the least challenging and the last the most demanding. Activity two must be slightly more difficult than the first, while the third activity must be closer to task four in its difficulty level. The first two activities must allow the students to engage with the same information in varied ways while the third and the fourth activities must make production demands on the mental faculties of the students. For example, the first activity can be a matching, or a choice activity as is presented in the image above. The second activity can be unfinished sentences with some parts present and some missing. The third activity can be one with no or minimal support for the students and asking them to produce information from their memory. The students, in similar ability groups, can be asked to choose one activity. It has been observed that students tend to choose activities which suit their ability levels voluntarily.

Once the structure has been revisited and brought to the fore front in the children's minds, a discussion on planning the content is called for. This debate can happen in similar capability groups where students now populate the sections of the essay that they have identified earlier. The teacher must visit each group while it's members are involved in discussion to ensure that they are on the right track as well as to give inputs where required. S/he might also be required to push the students to move ahead in case of a deadlock in the discussions ensues. Once such discussions are complete, the teacher can have a whole class discussion where students share their ideas and suggestions for the background information to be included, the theme statement, the positions that could possibly be taken along with their explanations and so on. With the end of this classroom conversation, the planning stage comes to a conclusion.

Other activities that can happen as a part of the planning stage are extra reading to populate the parts of structure, use of additional content organizers, visualization journeys conducted by the teacher to activate the student senses before they write a description, identify and collect the brick (subject content words related to the topic) and the mortar (linking words and expressions which are used to present the content words meaningfully in context) words and a whole class discussion on expressions or sentences starters and their structure which can be used to perform certain writing functions like expressing opinions, expressing a contrast, etc. Some of the questions that could be considered while discussing and planning the content are:

1. What will my audience want to know about my topic?
2. How can I best arrange my information?
3. What are the main ideas I want to present?
4. What details can I add to support my main ideas?
5. What will make a good lead to catch the reader's attention?
6. How can I end the piece effectively?

(JoAnn Miller, Editorial Macmillan, p. 3)

In fact, these questions can be the starting point of the debate on content.

### 1. Planning

Planning is the first and the most significant phase of the process cycle. This stage might be a time-consuming session and may spread over more than one day depending on the complexity of the text being taught and the ability of the students. A minutely planned and well-executed planning session can however, lead to time being saved in the following stages along with bringing in the added advantage of the students acquiring a long-term learning and understanding of the text type dealt with.

**2. Writing the First Draft**

Once the discussions and planning for the structure and content is complete, the next stage is writing the first draft. I believe that the first draft must be written by the groups that planned together. Each group can choose to appoint one scribe while the other members provide the inputs or divide the sections to be written by the different group members. These different sections can later be collated to be reviewed as one unit by the group.

The focus at this stage is only on the framing of the essay that has been meticulously and painstakingly planned for in the preceding hours; there is no focus on accuracy. At that time, it was just fluency.

**3. Editing**

Once each group has their first draft ready, the essay is passed to another group for a review. The teacher can decide the order of the passing around. The drafts can be collected by the teacher and redistributed making sure no group gets its own draft. Another way is to ask the groups to pass their drafts to the group next to them clockwise or anti-clockwise. At this time, the groups look at the drafts they receive for accuracy of structure and appropriateness of content as discussed. There might be differences in the positions the different groups take, the explanations offered, the theme statement or the evidence presented. All would be acceptable so long as they fulfil the basic criterion of suitability and are connected to the subject of the essay. So long as the structure is concerned, here there is more rigidity since the framework is fixed and variations will only make the presentation loose and scattered.

Editing and feedback go together. Groups study each other's drafts and scrutinize them for accuracy of structure and acceptability of content. The teacher can also choose to extend the analysis of the drafts for the language used, variety in diction, precision of grammar and the rightness of the linking words and expressions. S/he can either create a checklist with these aspects mentioned as items asking the students to tick as they edit or go back and forth between editing and feedback and drafting as many times as the number of elements to be examined. Another approach to editing is to further break down the areas of analysis and go slowly and step by step. For example, when checking for the correct use of the transition expressions, the teacher could first ask the groups to check the phrases or words that have been used for adding information to an already mentioned point, then move onto the expressions used for presenting a contrast and next to those used for exemplification and so on. The focus can be on the presence of the required language item as well as on its accuracy of use. This level of editing, however, is suitable to use with low ability students as with high capability students alone it will cause boredom and disinterest.

### 4. Writing the Final Draft

Once the text has been edited for all the areas that are important for academic achievement either in one round or multiple rounds, the final draft is written. This draft is written by each student separately as it reflects the individual assimilation that has happened over successive discussions, editing and feedback sessions.

The process approach is a time taking but effective method for teaching writing. Though the students may take much time when they are taken through the exercise the first time, with successive cycles they understand the workings of the activity and the time taken for the wheel to complete reduces significantly. Repeated exposure to the process pattern also hones their writing skills and prepares them for presenting various text types. Despite its efficacy, the process approach has received criticism from varied quarters and on a variety of fronts. Nunan (1991) mentions that the process writing approach has been criticized in that it confines children largely to narrative forms and places serious limitations on their ability to develop arguments, write reports and present expositions as demanded by academic circumstances. Roderigues (1985) states that the process writing approach presents an artificial writing scenario to the students. He says

> .... [Students] need structure, they need models to practise, they need to improve even mechanical skills, and they still need time to think through their ideas, to revise them and to write for real audiences and real purposes. (Nunan, 2015, p. 84)

Horowitz (1986) also criticizes this approach stating that it does not prepare students for examination writing. I would like to address all the above-mentioned criticisms by presenting another perspective to process writing. I agree that process writing does not present a simulated university or even school examination writing scenario to the students. However, let as look at this process as the exercise which develops students' writing skills and brings it to a level from where they can attempt examination writing with confidence and required knowledge of Academic expression. With regular and repeated practice students learn to edit their own work individually and with speed. They understand which areas to focus on for editing and how it impacts their presentation. Such training, in fact, prepares them for any kind of writing, be it academic or otherwise. Once the students have developed their writing skills, they can further work on their knowledge of the structure, language, and content of other texts with greater ease and speed. Let us look at process writing as the preliminary step to the product approach rather than as an exclusive methodology. For noteworthy results, we must use both the product approach as well as the process approach as complementary processes.

## The Product Approach to Teaching Writing

This approach works on the concept of emulating models of texts. It is most effective for learning to write texts which have a fixed structure and can be easily mimicked, for example, a laboratory report or a project report. These kinds of academic texts have an established and pattern, style and language as well as a set layout and content. There is not much creativity required for writing the mentioned texts. The theoretical underpinnings of this approach lie in the behaviourist approach to learning which said that learning is simply a matter of habit formation. With consistent practice, some actions or practices become habitual which we call learning. However, we could say that the product approach is very loosely based on the behaviourist theory since this theory primarily talks about the spoken skills related to a person's first language.

The product approach believes that students will learn to write a kind of text by carefully noticing its content, use of language, organization of grammar aspects and style (CLOGS), practising the areas which need more engagement and understanding before they can be reproduced, planning and organizing content for the aspired document and finally writing it. Let us look at each stage in detail and take the example of a lab report to further visualize the steps.

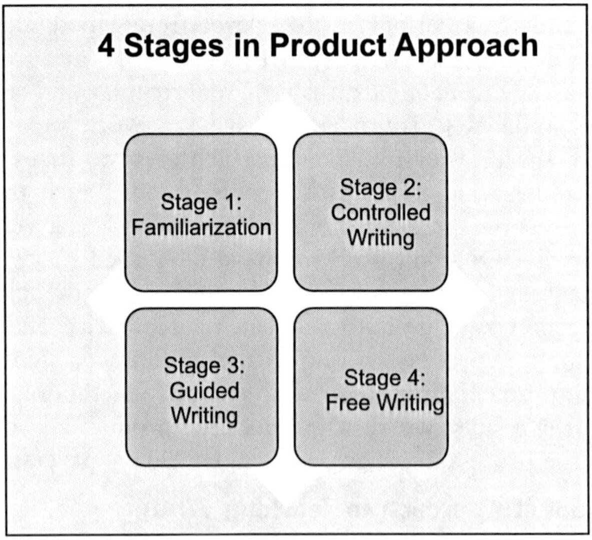


### Stage 1

The most important practice that adds value in learning by studying and reproducing a model text, is 'noticing'. This exercise is the crux of this stage. Here the teacher can provide a suitable and model sample of the text and ask the students to notice the CLOGS features of the text. The students can be asked to do so in pairs, groups or individually. In case groups are used, it is important to make mixed ability groups with one or maximum two strong learners. These learners automatically take lead and if required, can even break down the CLOGS features to simpler levels for assisted 'noticing' of the weaker students. In the beginning, the teacher might need to guide the students to break down the characteristics that require to be observed by asking guiding questions as the students look at the model text. Later with regular practice, students learn to do the same themselves.

### Stage 2

Once the students have been made to 'notice' the required aspects of the model text, the observation must be converted into learning through further and deeper interaction with the text features. At this juncture, the teacher must use a variety of activities to enhance the students' experience of the text. These tasks can be matching activities, gap fills, looking for examples, rearranging content, reordering headings, paraphrasing using synonyms or a different expression without a change in meaning, changing style from formal to informal in given statements, true or false, etc. The teacher can choose to focus on areas which s/he feels the students need further association with while keeping interaction with familiar facets of the text minimal or absent. While making groups for these activities, the teachers should be mindful of keeping similar ability students together to maximize impact. These activities make the students take their 'noticing' to the next level and their observation becomes knowledge. Equipped with a higher level of learning about the text and greater understanding of the features of the text, the students move into the next stage.

### Stage 3

In this stage, the students move from the model text to thinking about the text they are to produce. Having internalised the specific attributes of the desired text, the students start planning for the text they need to write. They are expected to place a special emphasis on matching the organization of traits and style while the grammar, use of language as well as the content might change slightly depending on the question or prompt that they are responding to. Students mostly plan this individually but may plan in groups or pairs as per the teacher's instructions and discretion.

**Stage 4**

This is the stage of the final draft. Students converge their erudition acquired through the previous stages into the writing of the final product here. They write individually. For feedback, students might be asked to compare their written text with the model text. Sometimes such comparison might highlight the need to go back to studying the model again, maybe with greater attention to the organization and structure.

The product approach has often been criticized for its tight control over the students' creativity and freedom to express. It has been lashed at for devaluing the writer's individuality and making him or her follow the beaten path mechanically. However, it is a popular approach to teaching writing in the academic arena. A comparative analysis of the two approaches to writing discussed above reveals how beautifully they complement each other, and one can predict their positive effectiveness if used together, one supplementing the other. While the process method develops confidence in writing in general, the product method takes the skill one step further and eases the students into an understanding of the various academic texts which have a defined structure, expected language use, predetermined style, demand for accuracy and mostly predictable content. Having said this, I would like to suggest that students be initiated into the arena of Academic writing through the process method in the lower and middle grades and later when they have overcome their fear of the genre and are no longer intimidated by it, their skills can be further honed through helping them master the diverse academic texts through the model mimicking method starting in the middle and continuing in the higher grades. I strongly recommend that the synergy between the two approaches be deployed in developing the Academic writing skills of the students in schools.

## Works Referred

Harmer, Jeremy. *How to Teach Writing*. Pearson/Longman, 2004.

Horowitz, Daniel. "Essay Examination Prompts and the Teaching of Academic Writing." *English for Specific Purposes*, vol. 5, no. 2, 20 June 2002, pp. 107-20. doi: https://doi.org/10.1016/08894906(86)90017-7 Get rights and content.

Kroll, Barbara. *Second Language Writing: Research Insights for the Classroom*. Cambridge University Press, 1993.

Langer, Judith A., and Arthur N. Applebee. *How Writing Shapes Thinking: A Study of Teaching and Learning*. National Council of Teachers of English, 1987.

Nunan, David. *Language Teaching Methodology: A Textbook for Teachers*. Prentice Hall, 1991.

"Writing." *Teaching English to Speakers of Other Languages: An Introduction*, by David Nunan, Routledge, Taylor & Francis Group, 2015, pp. 78-90.

# 8

# Referencing and Plagiarism

'Referencing' and 'Plagiarism' are two sides of the same coin and two of the most significant aspects of Academic writing. As a tenet of fair practice, referencing is the act of giving due credit to authors and researchers for their ideas, thoughts, findings, discoveries and explanations on which a writer bases or builds his or her hypothesis. It is the act of acknowledging the experiments and contributions of other minds in the field using which a writer supports his or her postulation and seeks to establish it as true. Referencing essentially involves accepting the influence of other works on the writer's thinking.

An academic essay is a repertoire of notions, concepts and inferences. It is important for the writer to reference so as to allow the reader to differentiate between the original ideas of the writer and those of other thinkers. Another reason that makes citations essential is that it allows the writer to showcase his or her widespread reading. It puts across to the reader that a wide range of perspectives, findings, thoughts, etc. has been considered by the author while writing the paper and this lends a higher level of credibility to the presentation. Referencing is also important for reasons of avoiding plagiarism. This concept will be discussed in greater detail later in the chapter.

There is a practical reason for referencing also which is to provide the necessary links to the reader in case s/he wants to carry out further research on an idea or theory that has been stated and drawn upon in a piece of Academic writing. A reader may also want to read the source of an idea mentioned in another written piece to analyse if the writer of the latter has interpreted the information accurately or appropriately. The overall purpose is just to establish an open environment and to suggest that the writer is open to discussions if required. It is, however, significant to point out that not everything needs to be referenced. Pieces of information like scientific truths, dates in history and facts of general knowledge need not be referenced. They are items of common knowledge. What must be referenced includes items of knowledge that are not common such as opinions, theories, statements and claims. The writer must also reference statistical date borrowed from other sources like graphs, information tables, financial tables, diagrams, etc. The primary reason for citing statistics is that different sources may state different figures.

Before a discussion on the format of referencing is initiated, it is imperative to establish how referencing is done in different written texts. While introducing a new perspective to an existing theory or proposing a variation or extension to an existing understanding of a concept or again presenting an altogether new hypothesis, researchers build their case by citing the ideas, research work, findings, etc. of other authors. Information or views expressed on websites, online or paper magazines or newspapers may also be used. They either quote the words of these writers verbatim or paraphrase their thoughts and opinions. Apart from the text, a writer may also use the statistics and date collated by another researcher or a diagram which represents information that supports the proposed idea. In all cases, the original thinker must be acknowledged and cited.

There are multiple styles that are followed to cite sources. For example, we have the MLA (Modern Languages Association) style; the APA (American Psychological Association) style; Chicago style and Harvard. Though there are others like American Sociological Association, Oxford Style, American Anthropological Association, IEEE and Vancouver Style, the ones mentioned earlier are most widely recognized and used. Schools and colleges adopt one style as the standard reference style and stick to it for all academic texts written and produced by their students through them.

The elements included in the process of referencing are essentially those that can help to locate a source. When reading or going through any reference material, the following are the elements that must be noted:

- **Who:** Author's complete name.
- **What:** Name of the book, article, website journal, magazine or any other source. Book title and page numbers when the item is a book chapter and journal title and page number when the item is a journal article.
- **When:** Date/year.
- **Where:** Publisher details as well as place of publishing. If it is a website the URL (Uniform Resource Locator) or DOI (Digital Object Identifier) and if it is an online journal then month and other release details

If we consider the sources of reference, there are normally four.

These are print books, online books or e-books, chapter in an edited book or an online journal article. Let us look at the minimum citation details needed for each.

### 1. Print Book

(a) Author's name(s)

(b) Title

(c) Year of publication

(d) Edition of the book (if applicable)

(e) Place where published

(f) Name of publisher

### 2. Online Book or E-book

(a) Author's name(s)

(b) Title

(c) Year of publication

(d) DOI or URL

### 3. Chapter in an edited book

(a) Author's name/s for chapter

(b) Title of the chapter

(c) Editor(s) of the book

**4. Title of Book**

(a) Page numbers of chapter
(b) Year of publication
(c) Place where published
(d) Name of publisher

**5. Online Journal Article**

(a) Author name/s
(b) Title of the ARTICLE
(c) Title/name of the JOURNAL in which the article is published
(d) Year of publication
(e) Volume number
(f) Issue number
(g) Page range
(h) DOI or journal homepage URL

The various citation styles simply present these pieces of information in a different order. References can be placed at different places in a text.

1. Immediately at the end of the reference, within the text. This is called in-text citation. Here the last name of the author along with the year of publication or the page number where one can find the cited matter is mentioned in brackets. At the end of the paper, or chapter a list of the works cited is presented. This is called the end of text citation. For example,

   "(Nunan 1991)" or

   "(Nunan. P. 87)"

   written at the end of a quote. Look at the example below

   CLIL is a generic term and refers to any educational situation in which an additional language, and therefore not the most widely used language of the environment, is used for the teaching and learning of subjects other than the language itself. (Marsh & Lange 2000)

2. Numbers are written next to the references in superscript and the complete reference for each number is provided in the footnote of the page on which the reference is given. Look at the image below to see an example of this kind of referencing.

1. First name Last name, Title of Book (Place of publication: Publisher, Year of publication), page number.
2. Antony Grafton, The Footnote: A Curious History (Cambridge, MA: Harvard University Press, 1999), 221.

https://www.scribendi.com/advice/what_are_footnotes.en.html

All the prominent referencing styles make use of either one of the two types mentioned above and place the pieces of information identified for each resource differently to be recognized as different styles.

The in-text citations call for further elaboration. In-text referencing happens for two kinds of content. One is a direct quotation, which is someone else's thought in the thinker's own words. The definition of CLIL given above as an example of a referencing pattern is also an example of a direct quotation. The other is a summary, which is someone else's idea in the writer's words. Look at the example below from the first chapter of this book:

> Speaking about Hyme's response, Marianne CelceMurcia, in her article, "Rethink the Role of Communicative Competence in language Teaching" says that while Chomsky believed that language could be learned free of a context, Hyme's believed that context was of prime importance. Not only must a learner understand the structure of language constructs but also how the same are used effectively.

There are two kinds direct quotations, short and long. The short quotation is of less that forty words and appears in the body of a paragraph. It is segregated with the help of quotation marks and followed by the name of the author and other information as dictated by the referencing style adopted by the writer. The long quotation appears as a separate body in the essay. It has an indent of five spaces and has no quotation marks. You will find examples of both in the book. A good rule of thumb is to avoid exceeding 5-10% direct quotations in a paper. A helpful and effective practice while in-text referencing is to cite the source as soon as you have written it in your essay, both in-text as well as end of text.

Having looked at in-text quotations, let us now look at summarizing as a way of referencing. Here an idea originally presented by someone else is mentioned by a writer in his or her paper in his own language. Though the language is the writer's the actual research is someone else's who must get the credit for it and hence citation becomes important.

The other part of citation is the end of text referencing. Here the complete detail about the referenced texts is given along with date and place of the publication. While the MLA format calls this list 'Works Cited', the APA calls it 'References'. However, both are the same and mention the texts referred to and cited in the alphabetical order of the authors' names. In case the author's name is unavailable, the name of the text is used. We often find another list at the end of texts, called bibliography. Bibliography is the list of books, journals, websites, articles from magazines or other sources which the author read to increase his understanding and knowledge about the topic itself. These works have been read but not cited in the research paper or essay. These works too are presented in an alphabetical order of the authors' names.

Let us look at some of the major referencing styles:

- **Modern Language Association Style**

MLA or Modern Language Association is a style of writing used for an advanced level of composition. It also denotes a referencing method developed for citations in research papers. MLA style is normally used in humanities-based courses such as Literature, History, and English. This style is used to give reference regarding books, journals, articles, websites, and anything else that students might refer to in their papers. It lays down rules for the formatting of the text and page layout. It also states rules for quotations that are used in the academic text as well as for the abbreviations that can be used in footnotes, endnotes etc.

For referencing, MLA 8th edition has laid out rules for 'in-text' as well as 'work cited' referencing. While 'in-text' referencing refers to writing the source immediately after the quote or paraphrase of a contribution from another author in the body of the essay or research paper, 'works cited' refers to citations given on a separate page at the end of the academic composition. As per MLA (8th edition), the last name of the author and the page must be mentioned. There is no punctuation between the name of the author and the page number. For example:

> CLIL is a generic term and refers to any educational situation in which an additional language, and therefore not the most widely used language of the environment, is used for the teaching and learning of subjects other than the language itself. (Marsh & Lange iii)

If the writer uses paraphrasing, for instance,

> Marsh and Lange (2000) define CLIL as a generic term that refers to any educational situation in an additional language, and therefore not the most widely used language of the environment. It is used for the teaching and learning of subjects other than the language itself.
>
> In the latter case only the page on which this thought appears is mentioned.

The source of the citations in the body of the text are mentioned in detail at the end of the paper as 'works cited'.

- **American Psychological Association**

MLA caters more to the needs of the humanities. A gap was felt in the sciences for a suitable referencing system. In 1929 a group of social and behavioural scientists sat together to put in place a set of simple standard rules for referencing in Academic writing in Science. It is normally used in term papers, research reports, empirical, scientific literature review, theoretical articles, etc. To elaborate, an academic paper on science is likely to include a variety of tables, diagrams, numbers and statistics, reports and abbreviations. To ensure a standard and consistent presentation of these to ease their comprehension, a style guide was needed which was put together by the American Psychological Association. As of today, most universities and some international schools use the APA for their referencing in science-based subjects like Psychology, Physics, Chemistry and so on.

This referencing style differs from MLA on some accounts. One is, as mentioned above, that what MLA calls works cited, APA calls 'References'. Another is that while making in-text citations, MLA just mentions the source and page no. with no punctuation, APA mentions the source, the date of publication as well as the page number(s) separated by a comma. So, the same quote on CLIL will be referenced as follows:

> CLIL is a generic term and refers to any educational situation in which an additional language, and therefore not the most widely used language of the environment, is used for the teaching and learning of subjects other than the language itself. (Marsh & Lange, 2000, p. iii)

Some similarities include use of quotes with short quotations and indented, long quotations with no quotes. Both the styles call for an alphabetical order of the referenced material.

- **Chicago**

This system of referencing was introduced in 1906 by the University of Chicago Press and specifically calls for the use of American English. It has released 17 editions so far. This style offers guidance on almost every topic including manuscript preparation, grammar usage and documentation and hence has been rightly called, the 'editor's bible'. This system of citation offers two methods of referencing—the Notes-Bibliography style and the Author-Date style. While the former is preferred by litterateurs, historians and scholars of the other arts, the latter is opted for by the practitioners of social and other sciences.

In the Notes-Bibliography system, every time the author either summarizes, paraphrases or quotes another thinker, a superscripted number is given. There is a note in the footnote section of the same page corresponding to each superscripted number in the text which provides all information (author's full name, source title, and details of publication) about the citation. It also allows the author to add a comment about the citation if required or desired. If the same source is mentioned again then the note only needs to include the surname of the author, a shortened form of the title (if more than four words), and the page number(s). This applies too in case the author chooses to include a Bibliography for each chapter. In fact, it is preferred to have a bibliography at the end of a text which catalogues all references, those that have been cited as well as those that provide for further reading on the topic. These texts are organized in an alphabetical order of the author's last name. In case no author's or editor's name is listed then the title of the text is referred to first.

The Author-Date system mentioned by Chicago entails the presence of the author's name along with the year of publication at the end of a quote, summary or paraphrase within the text. The same is applicable to a list of references at the end of the text with complete details. The format of presentation of a citation is the same in the Author-Date and the Note-Bibliography system.

We have briefly discussed the three most common styles of referencing used in schools for citation. I have not delved into the minute details of the referencing styles discussed since there are dedicated manuals and guides for each citation style easily available in the market and libraries. Therefore, only the basic and necessary information about the most used styles have been discussed. Though there are other important ones like Harvard, Oxford and even one that has been set by the Council for Science Editors, these have not been mentioned in detail given the fact that they are more popular in higher education than in schools.

## Plagiarism

Plagiarism is a serious offence in the academic world.

Plagiarism.org quotes the Meriam Webster online dictionary definition of the act of plagiarising as,

- to steal and pass off (the ideas or words of another) as one's own
- to use (another's production) without crediting the source

- to commit literary theft
- to present as new and original an idea or product derived from an existing source

Essentially plagiarism is an academic fraud. It entails using another person's thoughts, ideas, opinions, researches, findings and interpretations through diagrams and figures without acknowledging the contributor and giving him due credit. Small acts which might in some instances be a case of negligence and not deliberateness like missing quotation marks to indicate a contribution, giving incorrect information about the source of a quote or some data, presenting someone else's thoughts in one's own words without giving credit and the like also make for an act of plagiarism.

Nowadays, a lot of media items like videos, images and photographs are also used in academic presentations. Hence some areas where plagiarism also applies are the following:

- using a rehashed version of someone else's work or including clips from another video without mentioning the act of borrowing.
- using images like a photograph or scan to which another person has a copyright in one's own presentation without acknowledging it.
- creating an original video using copyright images or other media elements.
- Re-creating someone's work in one medium in another medium and calling it original.

In schools it is important to teach students how to avoid plagiarism. Academic honesty is a concept that is upheld and emphasized by most international academic boards and children are trained to maintain the highest level of honesty in their work. They are repeatedly advised to check their work for citations and unintended plagiarism.

Referencing is an important element of Academic writing. Though it has been addressed at the end of the book, its importance is high. It creates an atmosphere of positivity in the academic field where researchers are happy to be of use to each other. Thinkers do not mind their work being borrowed and used to build upon. They do not take offence when newer people challenge established perspectives and theories. This is all because, every time a researcher's work is cited, he or she gets recognition and eminence which is a pleasant feeling.

## Works Cited

"APA Style." *American Psychological Association*, American Psychological Association, apastyle.apa.org/.

Eisner, Caroline, and Martha Vicinus. *Originality, Imitation, and Plagiarism: Teaching Writing in the Digital Age*. University of Michigan Press, 2008.

Library. "Referencing Explained." *Library*, University of Leeds, 4 May 2017, library.leeds.ac.uk/info/1402/referencing/47/referencing_explained.

Pears, Richard, and Graham J. Shields. *Cite Them Right: The Essential Referencing Guide*. Macmillan International Higher Education/Red Globe Press, an Imprint of Springer Nature Limited, 2019.

University of Chicago Press Editorial Staff. *Chicago Manual of Style*. University of Chicago Press, 2017.

"What Is Plagiarism?" *Plagiarismorg RSS*, www.plagiarism.org/article/what-is-plagiarism.

www-Liby@waikato.ac.nz. "Library." *Referencing—The Library: University of Waikato*, www.waikato.ac.nz/library/study/referencing.

# 9
# Conclusion

Robert Fulton, the famous engineer and inventor who has been credited with the creation of the first commercially successful steam boat, once said, "The mechanic should sit down among levers, screws, wedges, wheels, etc. like a poet among the letters of the alphabet, considering them as the exhibition of his thoughts; in which a new arrangement transmits a new idea to the world". In the same way, a student seeking to acquire Academic language skills must engage and understand its component parts well, so that she or he can effectively synthesize the same in various combinations and produce meaningful texts of varied length and depth for different academic subjects. In this book I have highlighted the important elements that must be understood and internalized in a way that makes application of the learning active when required.

The book underlines the salient constituents of Academic writing like coherence and cohesion, register, tone, mood and style along with an understanding of the most common types of texts that one is expected to write in an academic context. The book elaborates on areas into which insight has been gained through careful study and observation, while those domains which have been addressed explicitly and in great detail in other sources, have been discussed in brief. The idea is to present this book as the root from which multiple branches come out and lead on to varied paths. The reader or researcher can choose to tread the path of his or her choice identified through understanding the status of current knowledge and pinpointing the areas in which there is need for further exploration. For example, the topic on types of essays has been laid out in much detail while the one on coherence and cohesion has not been taken up at such length because the latter topics have been much researched and there are specialists who have expounded the concepts in books dedicated to the same. For instance, Halliday has written a monograph on 'Cohesion' which is exhaustive in its treatment of the subject. Anyone who wishes to research on the topic can access the book referred to above.

In schools today, the product approach is most commonly adopted and practised to teach writing in different genres and to help and support students produce texts of varied kinds, academic and non-academic. The process approach has been relegated to the backyard maybe because it is more time consuming and requires a lot of meticulous planning. Exemplars or samples of varied text types can be used to refine the writing style and skills of the children in producing a certain type of text but using this method to teach writing amounts to stifling the individuality and creativity of the writer's original voice since emulating the sample provided is encouraged instead of developing the child's independent articulation skills. In my opinion, an appropriate and a more effective way of teaching writing is the process approach which must be begun at an early stage where the framework of text types does not exist. Once the child is proficient in writing in general, s/he can be schooled in genres and types of written forms.

When proposing this book as a resource for developing the Academic language skills of the students, I am assuming that the school will be open to the idea of promoting a system and culture of joint ownership. This implies that both the subject teachers as well as the English language specialists will together take the children of a grade through their journey of learning with alternate or joint focus on both content as well as language. As mentioned earlier, in the Indian context teachers of subjects other than English are not expected to have a high proficiency in English language even if that is the language of instruction of the school. So long as the teacher can communicate and put across the content knowledge, absence of knowledge about Academic English or even colloquial English is not noticed, rather not given much credence. In such a scenario, it is important that schools have language specialists who have a sound knowledge and understanding of Academic English and are equipped with appropriate and practical strategies and tools to be used to support language acquisition while studying subject content.

There are two ways in which the language specialist and the subject teachers can work in tandem. One is through taking turns in teaching and the other is through co-planning. Taking turns in teaching implies that while the subject teacher imparts subject knowledge, the language teacher makes the students focus on and acquire the language they must use in expressing their understanding and learning of the content taught. Once the subject teacher has finished teaching a section, the language teacher makes the children revisit the content with a focus on the language used to express the content. S/he might also focus on language functions or useful vocabulary that students might need to articulate their thoughts, ideas and erudition effectively in. The teachers can assess learning through a joint assessment which each teacher can scan for his or her teaching component. Though a separate assessment for both subject content as well as language is possible yet it is not viable because testing for language without content will not be reflective of the purpose.

The other and the more appropriate and effective method is collaborative planning for lessons. Both the language teacher and the subject teacher may plan for the reinforcement activities together to include emphasis on content as well as language. An option in this scenario is also to set multiple tasks, some which emphasize on language and others which lay stress on assessment of content. Care must be taken, however, that the language tasks present language in the context of the content being taught. Independent language tasks are not really effective.

When we talk of planning for teaching Academic language it involves diagnostic assessments, identifying gaps in knowledge and targeted teaching lessons. It also involves planning for identifying of appropriate and effective expressions used to present a position or claim and following the same up with an explanation, appropriate examples and a concluding thought. The teachers must also consider how the language as well as the content must be scaffolded for the low ability, ESL and special needs students. They must collaborate to anticipate knowledge gaps that might exist and consider how to bridge the same where the missing information is of utmost importance for the comprehension of and engagement with the content coming ahead. The teachers may also decide to let the gap be narrowed down by the students themselves by providing references and expecting self-study as they progress through to the next rung of the topic ladder.

This book brings to the forefront most of the areas which must be taught explicitly to the students for best results. Once the concepts involved are well understood, their application while writing for academic purposes is likely to become easier for the students. Teacher feedback might have more meaning and overall development may be more pronounced. However, it is up to the teacher to tie the loose ends that might exist in the knowledge and use of Academic language. Hence this book holds a higher value for the teachers themselves as it is they who will be able to put the blocks in position to create a meaningful image in the minds of their students.